FARROW&BALL®
LIVING with
COLOUR

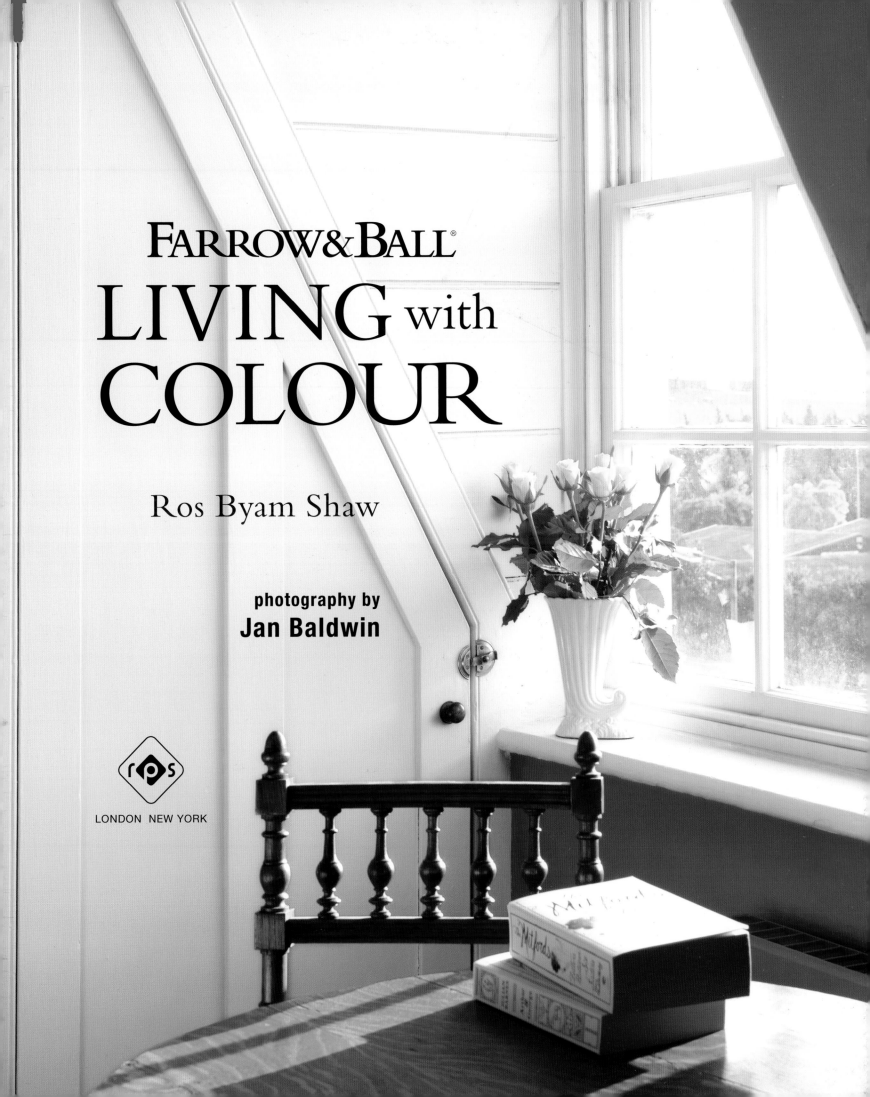

FARROW&BALL®
LIVING with
COLOUR

Ros Byam Shaw

photography by
Jan Baldwin

LONDON NEW YORK

This book is dedicated to Lydia.

Senior designer Toni Kay

Editor Delphine Lawrance

Location research Jess Walton
& Emily Westlake

Production Gordana Simakovic

Art director Leslie Harrington

Publishing director Alison Starling

First published in 2010
by Ryland Peters & Small
20–21 Jockey's Fields,
London WC1R 4BW
and
519 Broadway, 5th Floor
New York, NY 10012
www.rylandpeters.com

10 9 8

Text © Ros Byam Shaw 2010
Design and photography
© Ryland Peters & Small 2010

Library of Congress Cataloging-in-
Publication Data

Byam Shaw, Ros.
 Farrow & Ball living with colour /
Ros Byam Shaw. -- 1st US ed.
    p. cm.
 Includes index.
 ISBN 978-1-84975-038-7
 1. Color in interior decoration--Great
Britain. 2. Interior walls--Decoration--
Great Britain. I. Farrow & Ball. II. Title.
III. Title: Farrow and Ball living with
colour. IV. Title: Living with colour.
 NK2115.5.C6B93 2010
 667'.60941--dc22

                        2010014830

Printed and bound in China

RPS CICO BOOKS

For digital editions visit
rylandpeters.com/apps.php

*Please note that paint and
wallpaper colours may vary
due to the printing process.
We recommend using tester
pots and swatches to check
all colours in situ.*

CONTENTS

INTRODUCTION

This is a book about a particular kind of paint. It is about the company that makes this paint and about the people who choose it. It is also an exploration of what makes it unique and why it has such a loyal following. It shows how people have used it and the wallpapers that are made with it, in all manner of inventive and creative ways; in every style from poised minimalism to comfortable country house. Farrow & Ball is the company and its products are the common denominator in every story and photograph on the following pages.

Farrow & Ball paint is easy to spot even without the help of a label. First there are the colours: inimitable tones of off-white, stone and taupe, misty greys and blues, elusive greens, dusty pinks and so on for 132 shades of every stripe in the rainbow. Not one is harsh, obvious or bland. All are what you might call 'off-colours', knocked back and subtle – the sort you could stare at for a long time, colours you could happily set up home with. The same paint in the same choice of colours is used for the wallpapers, making them just as distinctive and instantly recognizable.

Much of Farrow & Ball's range is based on precedent – recreations of paint colours discovered during the restoration and conservation of historic buildings. Until the 18th century, when a wider choice of affordable pigments started to become available, colours came largely in the form of earth pigments such as ochre and umber. These formed the basis of the 'drab' palette typical of 16th- and 17th-century interiors, translated for modern use by Farrow & Ball into chic, fashionable neutrals such as 'String' or 'Olive'. By the 18th and 19th centuries

brighter blues, yellows, greens and reds were available and these too are reflected in the modern paints; 'India Yellow' for example, originally made by reducing the urine of cows fed on mango leaves, and 'Stone Blue', which was made using indigo.

Reviving period colours is a romantic notion that appeals to our fondness for the past and reverence for its aesthetics. But there is much more to Farrow & Ball than nostalgia. Their paints are equally appreciated by cutting-edge architects and

die-hard modernists, and can look as crisply contemporary as they can seem moodily historic. These are exceptional colours and cannot be successfully colour matched. A visit to the workshops in rural Dorset where the paints and wallpapers are made helps to explain why they are so difficult to copy. This is the site where in 1946 John Farrow and Richard Ball started to mix paints using traditional methods and ingredients. Forty years later the quality of their paints had become a rarity in a world dominated by vinyl emulsions. From a core of loyal customers looking for products suitable for the restoration of period interiors, word gradually spread to others who appreciated the lack of plastic additives and the handmade feel of the Farrow & Ball recipes.

Farrow & Ball is now global and the workshops and work force have expanded, but the original concept of old-fashioned craftsmanship and pride has never been compromised. Ingredients are sourced from the same trusted suppliers and include iron oxides that have been used as pigments since prehistoric times, lime putty, chalk, linseed oil, china clay and siliceous earth. Not only are the ingredients consistently high quality, the paints contain up to 30% more pigment than most other brands. It is this high level of pigment, suspended in a rich resin binder without the usual 'filler' of microscopic acrylic beads, plus the refractory qualities of titanium dioxide, that make it so difficult to replicate a Farrow & Ball paint. The chemistry is complex, but the result is plain to see. Farrow & Ball paints have a depth that seems to draw the eye in 'almost as if you could dip your hand into the wall', as one employee describes it.

Technology is used to ensure that each batch of a particular colour is precisely matched to a standard twice as accurate as that commonly used by the paint industry. Environmentally, Farrow & Ball is equally ahead of industry standards. All of its paints are water based, and are each classified as having either low, minimal or zero VOCs (volatile organic compounds). In practice, this means that the paints have very little odour and there are no potentially harmful emissions as they dry.

Farrow & Ball wallpapers are as unique as the paints they are made with, and because their colours are the same as the paint colours, they can be seamlessly coordinated with paintwork in a room scheme. Designs are adapted from archives, whether the simple 'Polka Square', taken from the background of an 18th-century paper, or the fabulous 'Wisteria', translated from a 19th-century fabric. All patterns have a painted ground, applied using brushes, and designs are either block printed or trough printed onto it, adding another layer of texture and contributing to the rich, handcrafted character of the papers.

Famous for their quality, Farrow & Ball paints are almost as famous for their names. While many are descriptive, 'Fawn', 'Blue Gray', 'Off-Black', and others such as 'Joa's White' and 'Calke Green' refer to people or houses, a significant minority are memorably odd. 'Dead Salmon' is probably best known, but there are also 'Mouse's Back', 'Elephant's Breath', 'Ointment Pink', 'Churlish Green', 'Smoked Trout', 'Cat's Paw', 'Matchstick' and 'Bone'. The names themselves are a tradition, and whenever a small number of new colours replace existing colours in the 132-strong chart, there is a meeting to discuss what they should be called.

As for how to use these evocatively named, carefully made paints and wallpapers, it is reassuring and possibly a little daunting to know that there are no strict rules. Colour is a matter of personal preference, as is pattern, and who knows whether the shade of green one perceives is exactly the same as that seen through another person's eyes? There are, however, guidelines to minimize the possibility of getting it wrong. Before making a decision, it is helpful to buy sample pots of the colours that you are considering and use them to paint a large piece of card that you can move around a room in order to see the colour in different lights. It can also be useful to know whether a colour has a warm or a cool tinge. Cool colours should generally be avoided in north-facing rooms, as the effect can be too chilly for comfort.

The houses featured on the following pages offer inspiration, as do the swatches at the end of each colour chapter, although it should be noted that colour accuracy cannot be guaranteed due to the printing process and variations in light during photography. If you remain unsure of what goes with what, there is help available, either on Farrow & Ball's website, through their stockists or at a Farrow & Ball showroom where trained colour consultants can advise you in person.

Paint is the least expensive way to transform a room. And, unlike knocking down a wall or tiling a floor, it is not difficult to rectify if you have made a mistake. Colour should be fun; at its best it is joyful. 'Why do two colours, put one next to the other, sing?' asked Picasso. 'Can one explain this? No. Just as one can never learn to paint.' Even Picasso didn't understand how colour works. But it didn't stop him using it.

Ros Byam Shaw

PART ONE

STYLES

The 16 homes featured on the following pages are grouped according to broad stylistic definitions and range from a compact city apartment to a capacious mini-mansion in the middle of the countryside. The way they have been furnished and decorated is as heterogeneous as their architecture, but two common factors link these hugely varied interiors: first, all have that elusive and enviable quality that is innate style, and second, all have been decorated using Farrow & Ball paints and wallpapers.

CLASSICAL

With its shutters and panelling, cupboards and cornices, an 18th-century interior cries out for paint. Whether streamlined by the use of a single matt colour or highlighted in subtly different tones, Georgian woodwork comes to life under a coat of good-quality emulsion. From the shades of 'drab' and off-white that characterized the early years of the period, to the bold, bright contrasts of the Regency, the painted walls and woodwork in these period houses show Farrow & Ball's authentic colours and finishes at their elegant best.

LEFT *The panelling, architraves, doors and even the stair risers in the hall of William Palin's early 18th-century London townhouse are painted in 'Light Stone', an archive colour available to order. The colour was suggested by conservation architect Julian Harrap, and would have been considered appropriate by the first owners of the house at a time when entrance halls were often painted in shades of stone. The ceilings are in 'New White' and a glimpse of the dining room in dusky 'Calke Green' can be seen to the right of the hall.*

RIGHT *Double doors link the first floor drawing room at the front of the house and the study at the back. The colours of each room, 'Octagon Yellow' and 'Book Room Red', meet in a neat line down the leading edge of the doors. William is delighted by the way the colours contrast and relate.*

BELOW *The exterior of the house is painted in two modest shades of off-white: 'Biscuit' for the door and shutters, 'Light Stone' for the window frames and glazing bars. They are both archive colours and are typical of the period when the house was built.*

PANEL GAME

Architectural historian William Palin has rescued and revived two classical houses, both of which are featured in this chapter of the book. One was built at the beginning of the 18th century when classicism was still a relatively new import to this country, the other dates from the first quarter of the 19th century when classicism was about to be overtaken by gothic as the most fashionable architectural style. Both houses glory in a rainbow of magnificent Farrow & Ball colours.

RIGHT *William had photographs
that helped him reconstruct the
panelling in the ground floor dining
room, which had been stripped out in
the 1980s. 'Calke Green' was, he says,
his 'first move away from the early
Georgian sand-based palette. I wanted
something strong and dark to create a
sense of transportation and seclusion –
a place where guests would lose track
of time. Prints look perfect against the
green and with candles it becomes an
enchanting and theatrical space.'*

BELOW *Defying Georgian
convention, William moved the kitchen
up from the basement to the ground
floor where it adjoins the dining room.
Glass bottles in bright jewel colours
catch the light on the rail of a sash
window painted 'Dorset Cream'.*

This is the earlier house, dating from 1717, in London's
Spitalfields – an area colonized throughout the 18th-
century by refugee Huguenot silk weavers. It has
been a Mecca for lovers of Georgian architecture
since the 1970s when a few bold pioneers moved
into the run-down streets, lured by the original 18th-
century features of these once prosperous terraces,
features that later occupants had always been too
poor to rip out and update. William's mercy mission
began in 1997 when he bought the house in a state
that he fondly describes as 'picturesque decay'.

Black and white photographs taken in 1971 and
now hanging in the faultlessly restored hall and stairs
show an interior of Dickensian shabbiness; cracked
lino on the stairs and a stone sink in a corner of a
landing. The attic looks particularly squalid, even
in romantic monochrome, with a bulging ceiling and
buckets beneath holes in the roof.

Things had improved in some respects by the time
William first saw the house. Sadly, however, all the
panelling visible in the photographs had disappeared
– ripped out and sold in the period feature frenzy
of the 1980s. Replacement features included a tree
trunk complete with bark and branches propping up
a lower flight of stairs, an inspired if inappropriate
flourish of DIY invented by the young couple who
were living there in bohemian semi-dereliction.

Despite the mess and the lack of panelling, William
was charmed by what he calls 'the delicate, creaking
fragility' of this modest, five-storey townhouse. 'It
had a special atmosphere,' he says, 'a combination of
the fine proportions of the rooms and the fragments
of surviving woodwork and early decoration. In the
attic and basement, which had been uninhabited
for years, there were layers of historic paint on the
peeling walls – from dove greys to sumptuous deep
greens. I didn't want to lose this magic.'

A self-proclaimed 'obsessive' about early Georgian
London, William was taking an MA in Architectural
History when he bought the house. He has since
worked for The Georgian Group and Sir John Soane's
Museum, and is currently Secretary of SAVE Britain's
Heritage. He had the knowledge and connections to

be the ideal knight in shining armour for this building in distress, and is full of praise for those who helped him. Among them are architect Julian Harrap; the joiners who put new panelling in rooms that over the years had sagged and sloped; Trevor Barnes, 'the only man in London, possibly the world, who really enjoys working with floorboards.'

Between them, these experts and craftsmen gave back to the house everything it had lost, from pine panelling and floorboards, to shutters and glazing bars. Julian Harrap had already suggested Farrow & Ball for the rooms and shared what William calls his 'architectural rather than purely decorative' approach to paint colour. 'Unfurnished panelled rooms have a wonderful, poetic purity and beauty, and I was eager not to disrupt this, which is why I decided to use one colour floor to ceiling for the panelling in each room and why I have tried not to clutter the spaces with too much furniture.'

As a result of William's sensitivity, the house has kept its magic. The entrance hall, painted 'Light Stone', the warm white of vanilla ice cream, opens into a 'Calke Green' dining room; a dark, slightly mysterious colour which suits a room that comes to life for dinners by candlelight. On the floor above, the front room is a punchy mustard ('Octagon Yellow') and the study that adjoins it is 'Book Room Red', like the juice from a summer pudding mixed with cream. Next floor up is the 'Stone Blue' bathroom, and then, at the very top, there is the beautiful, surprising space of the old weaver's loft with its long run of windows along the front and back of the house. With views over a disused brewery on one side and the roofs of Georgian Spitalfields on the other, this room has the safe, remote feel of an ancient wooden ship floating on top of an urban wave. This is William's bedroom and has 'Pea Green' walls. 'This colour helps to build a sense of intimacy,' he says. 'And helps transport the mind.'

ABOVE *In the drawing room, William opted for 'Octagon Yellow', which he describes as 'a particularly beguiling colour – changing dramatically under different light levels – appearing grey or even green depending on the quality of light'. The bookcase is painted in 'Mahogany'.*

ABOVE LEFT *Although the panelling had gone, the 1717 staircase was nearly intact. William left the stair treads unpainted and used 'Mahogany' for the rail and balusters, 'slopped on joyfully by my decorators with minimal preparation so as not to eradicate all the scars and wear of the past 300 years'.*

RIGHT *William calls the bathroom 'a bit of fun' and says, 'As bathrooms are a modern invention "Stone Blue", strong but slightly contemporary in feel, seemed perfect, and at last I had somewhere to put Blur's baby in a bathtub.' (Poster by Stylorouge).*

PERFECTLY PLAIN

Designer George Carter is a jack of all trades and a master of them too. Not only did he design the garden, extension, internal architecture, joinery and interior décor of this pretty red brick house in Norfolk for long-term clients who have become firm friends, he also found the house for them. 'They are based in London,' he explains, 'but were looking for a weekend house in the country. I had admired this house for ages. It isn't very grand from outside, but it is neat and self-contained, with a walled garden and shutters; the kind of house that is easy to close up and leave.'

ABOVE *George Carter's restoration of the house has helped to link it more closely with its pretty walled garden at the rear. The bench and chair are painted in 'Green Smoke', one of George's favourite colours for garden furnishings, the windows frames, door and guttering are in 'Shaded White' and the soil pipe is appropriately painted in 'Down Pipe'.*

LEFT *The kitchen is deliberately designed to provide a plain, unified background to the clutter that inevitably accumulates in any well-used space, and has units painted in 'Off-White' and walls and ceiling in 'Lime White'. The floor is a pale lino, the surfaces pale Corian and the splashbacks are transparent glass.*

George Carter saw potential in the house that wasn't immediately obvious to less practised eyes. Dating from 1840, which according to George is still Regency in Norfolk because they were a bit behind the times, it was built for the land agent of a nearby estate and has a single-storey annexe that was the original office. George describes it as 'what Jane Austen would call the smallest house that could rank as genteel, as it had miniature stables, a groom's room, a separate staircase to a tiny bedroom for a single maid and two good front rooms looking up the village street'. The client saw something a little less romantic. 'It was a bit of a mess,' she admits, 'but we both have total confidence in George's judgement, knowledge and vision, and we knew he would make it lovely.' Which is exactly what he has done.

George's most significant innovation was to gather the messy bits at the back of the house, including the scullery, the groom's room and the maid's room, all under one roof, and to give the resulting single-room extension a high ceiling and a gracefully bowed back wall with tall windows and French doors opening into the garden. 'Without this addition, none of the downstairs rooms would overlook the garden, which would be a great shame,' explains George. With it, the house is allowed to breathe. While the smaller, more formal front rooms have a modestly proportioned elegance, the rear living room that now embraces the garden room extension is bright, light, spacious, and almost summery even on a dull winter afternoon.

In addition to the building of the new extension, the interior of the house needed reconfiguring to provide an adjoining bathroom for the main bedroom and to promote the symmetry and proportion that are integral to George Carter's brand of restrained classicism. In the annexe he made an arched entrance to match the arched alcove on the other side of the

chimney breast. The paired columns that flank the opening into the garden extension and are necessary structurally are another Georgeism, as is the exterior leadwork to the oriel window. These are both examples of what he calls 'making posher' that have helped lift the house from attractive to utterly charming.

ABOVE *Where once there was a mess of small rooms, George has built a single garden room with a curved back wall and French doors leading into the garden. Classical pillars flank the opening into this new space and are structural as well as decorative, their subtle paint finish applied by Paola Cumiskey. Walls and woodwork are in 'Slipper Satin'.*

LEFT *A simple trestle table in the garden room means it can be used for summer dining or as a light-filled study on a dark winter afternoon. Highlights of green enhance the airy, sunny atmosphere.*

RIGHT *At the front of the house are the two original reception rooms. George has lined the dining room with bookshelves painted in 'Off-White'. 'Off-White' has also been used for the walls, which helps to make the bookcases feel integral to the architecture of the room.*

The same level of restraint informs the palette of colours George has chosen for walls and woodwork, in the shades of neutral that he favours as a background for pictures and furnishings. 'I have used Farrow & Ball paints ever since they first appeared,' he says. 'They have a knocked-back quality that gives them a complex, period feel.' Ever inventive, George also uses paint to give instant character to new wood and to unify his furniture creations, such as the old desk in the garden room for which he designed a top with panelled doors and shelving. 'We painted the whole thing in dragged "Pavilion Gray" and then matt glazed it to homogenize the effect.' Picture frames have been given a coat of 'Off-White', rubbed with wire wool and then waxed. Even the wooden Venetian blinds in the bathrooms are in Farrow & Ball paints to match.

The neutral palette is spiced up with jolts of colour in the living rooms and bedrooms: apple green upholstered chairs in the garden room; a scarlet cushion in the dining room and library that picks up the red spines of books in the floor-to-ceiling shelving; a strawberry pink chair in the main bedroom; a turquoise lamp base here, a richly patterned needlework cushion there.

Most determinedly neutral of all of the room schemes is the kitchen, which has walls and ceiling in 'Lime White', joinery and windows in 'Off-White', splashbacks in clear glass, surfaces in creamy Corian and on the floor a lino almost exactly the same pale

shade. 'Kitchens tend to get full of stuff,' George opines, 'but a single-colour background helps to stop the room becoming too cacophonous.' Conversely, stronger colour is allowed in bathrooms; 'Babouche' in the cloakroom and 'Gervase Yellow' in the house bathroom, because here, says George, 'there are few other opportunities to introduce colour, and you are not having to look at it all the time.'

LEFT *In one of the spare bedrooms, walls, skirting, architrave and the door of the fitted cupboard have all been painted in 'Buff', a pale brown chosen for its warmth in a north-facing room. 'I only use the cooler neutrals in rooms that face south,' says George.*

ABOVE *Having divided the main bedroom to make an adjoining bathroom, George designed wall panelling to restore a sense of proportion and painted it in 'Skimming Stone' with walls above it and ceiling in 'Cornforth White'. Frosted glass panes in the door provide privacy and extra light.*

THIS PAGE *Bathrooms are the only rooms in a house in which George likes to use strong colours because, as he says, there are few other opportunities to introduce colour and because you are only looking at the colour for relatively short periods of time. In this bathroom he has chosen 'Gervase Yellow' and hung botanical prints with frames painted in 'Off-White'.*

For some people, the presence of workmen in their home is a necessary evil, made bearable only by the prospect of years of undisturbed privacy, having showers in the new bathroom, eating breakfast at the new island counter or shutting teenagers in the loft conversion. For others, a workman is a fine thing: a representative of change, a companion in creativity. These are the people for whom moving house is a happy hobby.

ARTFUL MIX

The owner of this late 18th-century terraced house in South London falls into the latter camp. She and her husband moved in two years ago, making this house number 18 of their married life together. It is still a work in progress and there is at least one resident workman, 'wonderful Martin', the carpenter who has restored their panelling, built their fitted cupboards and mended their sash windows and pull-up shutters. 'I quite enjoy doing up houses,' she admits, with more than a whiff of understatement. 'Our three children have all left home, but they do sometimes ask us, "When are you moving again?" And I say, "Not for the moment", but maybe when five floors get too much we will start looking around.'

LEFT *The lower ground floor of this late Georgian townhouse has been opened up to make a single room with the working end of the kitchen at the front and a large sitting and dining room at the back where a door leads into the garden. The floor is pale limestone and the bright, spacious feel is enhanced by walls in 'Pointing' and ceilings in 'All White'. Contemporary and vintage furnishings look all the more chic for their period setting.*

RIGHT *The kitchen units were inherited from the former owners and have been re-painted rather than replaced, using 'Teresa's Green' for the floor units to match the fitted cupboards on either side of the fireplace at the other end of the room.*

She describes this latest move as 'downshifting and upsizing'. 'We were living in Kensington and prices were so ludicrous that we effectively swapped our house there for a smaller house in Kensington that we rent out and this much bigger house that we live in.' Her husband is French and a lawyer. They also have a house in Paris and he commutes weekly between the two cities. 'Sometimes I go with him, but usually I stay as I work at the Tate Britain and Tate Modern art galleries as a volunteer guide and also one day a week as an archivist in the photographic library at the Royal Institute of British Architects,' she says.

Their attraction to this particular house was a slow burn. 'We first saw it online when our daughter was house-hunting and we rather fell in love with it. But we pulled back because of its location, which is so much less central than we were used to and with no tube nearby. Two years later, our younger son was looking for property and saw that the house was on the market again. The young couple who had bought it had started a family and wanted to move to the country. We came to see it and I looked out of the drawing room window, across gardens to the churchyard and said, "Isn't this enough country for you?", but then I am someone who gets nervous when there isn't a pavement.'

The appeal of the house is obvious; well-proportioned, high-ceilinged rooms spread over five floors, the charm of original fireplaces and panelling and the bonus of an elegantly bowed

ABOVE RIGHT *In the main bedroom, the antique overmantel is French and the wall light was carved by a craftsman in Venice.*

RIGHT *In the same room, the metal four-poster bed, which was made for the owners in the South of France, faces a curved wall and a trio of sash windows overlooking gardens towards a churchyard. The wall colour above the panelling is 'Borrowed Light', with 'Slipper Satin' used below and also on the rails of the door panelling. The rest of the woodwork is 'White Tie' and the ceiling is 'All White'.*

LEFT *The small ground floor sitting room at the front of the house has an unusual marble and stone fireplace and original panelling. The owner has chosen to draw attention to the panelling by painting it 'Oval Room Blue' above a skirting in 'White Tie' and below walls in 'Slipper Satin'. Darker colours used below lighter shades on the lower section of walls have the effect of grounding a room.*

back wall, which gives the big rooms at the rear of the house views in three directions from the triple sash windows that curve across it. 'It is a very spacious, comfortable house,' the owner acknowledges. 'My husband has a whole floor to himself and when my son and grandchild come over from America they can also have their own floor at the top of the house.'

Being a serial mover brings the advantage of having made repeated tries to find the trusted. These owners have an address book of workmen they know and like, and of sources for everything from door handles to paint. 'We have used Farrow & Ball paints in several houses,' she says. 'In Paris we have "Blackened", which is a lovely soft grey, and we have also used it here in the top bedroom, where it works beautifully with "Incarnadine", which is a nice, rosy red. We have also chosen several Farrow & Ball colours for this house that I have never tried before – "Saxon Green" for the panelling in the first floor bathroom, and "Oval Room Blue" for the same panelling in the sitting room on the floor below. Darker, more

LEFT *On the floor above the sitting room is the master bathroom with the same original wall panelling, here painted in 'Saxon Green', contrasting with walls in 'Pointing'. When the carpet was stripped out, the owners found the original deal floorboards beneath. Their 'wonderful carpenter' restored the pull-up shutters.*

masculine colours seem to suit this type of woodwork. It draws your eye to the detail and grounds the room if you use a lighter colour on the walls above.'

An eye for colour has led the owners to be subtle and inventive. In the main bedroom, paint disguises missing sections of the flat wall panelling and highlights architectural details. Doors are a slightly darker shade of white than architraves, giving a more three-dimensional quality, and the dado rail is lighter than the flat panelling below it. 'If you use too many shades of the same colour to pick out every moulding it can look a little twee,' the owner muses. 'I like to use paint to create an effect that is satisfying but not consciously noticeable.'

ABOVE *The top floor of the house is an early 19th-century extension and now provides guest bedrooms and a bathroom. The owner was thrilled to discover 'Incarnadine', which she describes as a 'nice, rosy red that goes beautifully with the ceiling and woodwork in "Blackened", which is a lovely soft grey.'*

Sheerness is one of those strange, forgotten places with the mournful appeal of past greatness, now swamped by roundabouts, supermarkets, semi-industrial buildings and post-war housing estates. At the tip of the Isle of Sheppey, where the Thames broadens into the sea, the docks of Sheerness were once the most advanced naval installation in the world. Developed between 1813 and 1840, they included a series of splendid homes and terraces that were built to house Royal Navy officers who were stationed in the area.

NAVAL HISTORY

In the 1960s the Admiralty sold the dockyard. Only two of the Regency terraces survived demolition, defiantly handsome, and now saved for posterity thanks to recognition by the World Monument Fund. In one of these terraces is the second home of architectural historian and Secretary of SAVE Britain's Heritage, William Palin.

William Palin's first home is in Spitalfields and it was through his association with the Spitalfields Trust, another organization devoted to the preservation and protection of historic buildings, that he discovered this isolated pocket of architectural beauty. He bought the house in 2007, attracted by its remarkably original condition, a quality irresistible to the

ABOVE *The house forms part of a terrace, built in 1824 for naval officers. This terrace just outside the dock wall was for 'inferior' officers, although the houses are large nonetheless. The front door and the railings are painted in 'Trust Green'.*

LEFT *William has used refined versions of all the primary colours throughout the house creating what he calls an 'episodic effect' as you move from room to room. For this room he chose punchy 'India Yellow' in casein distemper, a finish that he says has 'a wonderful organic feel'. The fitted cupboard is in 'Mahogany', and like all the joinery in the house, the finish is dead flat oil, which William loves for its 'creamy, tactile surface'. The idea for the two-tone skirting in 'Off-Black' and 'Old White' came from a Regency painting of an interior belonging to William's neighbours.*

RIGHT *The basement kitchen and dining room are in 'Lime White' and the fireplace, the skirtings and the fingerplates on the cupboard doors are 'Off-Black', the latter detail copied from original examples found on the back of some of the doors, designed to hide coal-covered servants' fingerprints.*

LEFT *At the front of the house on the raised ground floor, the study has walls painted 'Book Room Red', again in casein distemper. This warm terracotta looks almost brown in some lights and combines with the brighter red of the antique turkey carpet and the dark polished mahogany of the antique furnishings to create a look that is rich, dignified and masculine. William has used the same colour for one of the attic bedrooms where the effect is more intimate than grand.*

RIGHT *The semi-basement has unusually high ceilings and large windows for a part of the house once the sole reserve of servants. Light is maximized by William's choice of 'Lime White' throughout. The baskets, reclaimed earthenware sink and plain open shelving contribute to the simple, old-fashioned feel of the room.*

true enthusiast. The house dates from about 1824 and William's description of it as both 'grand and simple, with stripped-down Grecian classical detailing – nothing too fussy for the officers' sums up its appeal. Unlike his house in Spitalfields, where he re-introduced lost period features such as panelling, this house had retained its shutters, fireplaces, cornices, floorboards, and even fitted cupboards 'just like in a ship', as William notes.

Blessed with interiors that were architecturally complete, with no need for curtains thanks to the shutters and unhindered by furniture (which he has only gradually acquired since), paint and colour were William's priority. Having been introduced to Farrow & Ball paints by the architect Julian Harrap who worked on the restoration of William's early Georgian house in London, he already had certain favourites; colours such as 'Light Stone', 'Pea Green', 'Book Room Red' and 'Octagon Yellow', which he decided to use again. But he was also inspired by another house in the terrace restored to Regency splendour by its owners, headmaster Howard Fisher and piano teacher Justin Webb. 'Justin is the old house boffin and has a working 1800s kitchen with a clockwork spit in his basement!' William smiles. 'He helped source many of the missing details for my house, such as locks, bell-pulls and so on.'

Not only did William copy some of the colours used by these excellent neighbours, such as 'Lime White' in the basement and 'Mahogany' for the stair banisters, he also managed to persuade them to do the painting. 'The two of them painted the entire house top to bottom, carefully, sensitively and with amazing results,' William enthuses. 'Howard, being over 6ft [1.8m], specialized in ceilings and walls; Justin worked exclusively on joinery. They still curse me for my radiators. Howard says each one took four hours to paint.' In keeping with the period of the house, they used dead flat oils for the woodwork and joinery. Most of the walls and ceilings are painted in distemper.

William is right to say that the results of their labours are 'amazing'. The different colours used throughout, from the fresh white kitchen and dining room in the basement, to the sky blue bathroom at the top of the house, with a yellow drawing room, a red study and a green bedroom in between, give the house what William calls an 'episodic quality – the experience of wandering from one strongly painted room to another – each affording different internal and external views and vistas.' He also describes the excitement of visiting the house as it was being decorated and 'witnessing these generously proportioned, modestly detailed rooms come to life under blankets of colour.'

Furnishings, which William has variously bought from antiques shops, eBay and a Sheerness house clearance auction almost opposite his front door, are purposely sparse. 'I have always been careful not to over-fill the rooms and this allows the painted surfaces to dominate,' he explains. 'I have very few "special" things. It's mostly junk, apart from the clocks, which I buy from my uncle who is an architect, and those are special.'

ABOVE AND RIGHT *William recycled many of the colours he had already used in his London house, including 'Pea Green', which he has also used for his bedroom in the old weaver's loft in his house in Spitalfields. It is a colour he finds both intimate and contemplative, although its effect in different spaces is surprisingly dissimilar: elegant in this tall, beautifully proportioned first floor room; quirky in the Spitalfields attic. Being a favourite, William has used 'Pea Green' again in a top floor bedroom (right).*

LEFT *William recycled many of the colours that he had already used in his London house, including strong 'Stone Blue' for the bathrooms. He regards this as a colour with a modern feel, even though it is based on an 18th-century distemper, originally made with indigo. Here, as elsewhere in the house, he has used 'Old White' for the woodwork, which he says 'has a sort of ready-weathered look.'*

William Palin is as modest in manner as he is in his approach to interior decoration. He is also witty, a very good mimic in the family tradition and far more likely to tell a funny story against himself than, for example, mention the many exhibitions he put on at Sir John Soane's Museum in London where he was Assistant Curator. He is, however, pleased with his work of restoration and decoration. 'I like to think that this house is like a piece of theatre. I wanted to use colour to create variety, change, surprise and excitement, while bringing out the intrinsic dignity of the spaces.'

CITY

The country versus city debate rumbles on; pavements or fields, culture or cows, shopping or

shooting. Different ways of living inspire different styles of interior. City homes tend to be sharper

and more chic. Space and time are more precious, so furnishings must earn their place; style and

fashion are more apparent and so seem more important. And since there is a lot less mud,

it is possible to keep white painted floors clean, as Jo Berryman does in her fashion-conscious

Hampstead home, one of three slick city interiors on the following pages.

Most owners of beautiful interiors have horror stories to tell; the dirt, the damp, the squatters, the builders, the dust, the disasters and the hideous décor they were unfortunate enough to inherit. All offer the attraction of *schadenfreude* and the satisfaction of a happy ending. But Conrad Roeber and David Townsend's horror story has an added ingredient: the fascination of extreme eccentricity.

HIGH DRAMA

Their flat is one of those surprising oases sometimes found in central London. On the corner of a Soho street, the entrance is anonymous and easy to miss. Once inside the tiny hall there is a steep staircase to the very top of this four-storey building. Behind their front door is yet another staircase. As you climb it you pass a window and a curtain of ivy that drops from above as if some leafy giantess had thrown her mane of hair over the edge of the roof.

Ahead is a glass door onto a decking terrace fringed with more greenery. In the other direction, the hallway landing leads straight into a single, large room, its ceiling open to the rafters and its row of windows looking out onto gables, rooftops and sky.

LEFT *Conrad and David opened the main room of their fourth floor flat into the rafters, where a previous occupant had bizarrely squeezed in a bedroom. A more comfortable bedroom and bathroom protrude into the room, the walls of which are painted 'Hardwick White' in a continuation of the open entrance hall to the left. The window wall is a darker shade of grey, 'Chemise'. Despite appearances, no bright white has been used. The ceiling is 'Strong White' and the beams and woodwork are the slightly darker 'Cornforth White'. The kitchen door fronts are tin, rusted by a combination of sulphuric acid and rain.*

RIGHT *Leading off the entrance hall are the main bedroom and bathroom. The angled wall of the bathroom is painted deep, dark 'Hague Blue' as a means of giving architectural integrity to a space that has been carved out of the corner of the larger room.*

Thanks to its elevation and the muffling effect of double glazing, the space is as quiet as it is voluminous. A sophisticated colour scheme of grey, brown and charcoal, like a chic black and white photograph, is punctuated by a single bright red disc, a painted machine mould propped on a shelf against a wall hung with monochrome paintings.

Poised, comfortable, with a log fire burning in a sharp, contemporary fire surround made from rusted metal, it is impossible to imagine what a strange and unappealing space this was when Conrad and David first viewed it. Taking it in turns to describe the scene, they explain that the flat had been occupied by a single man who had barely furnished it but had planned to build a lunar clock on its roof. The water in the lavatories was black, as the mains supply had been turned off because of a leak, but odder still was the owner's bedroom, a space above the ceiling in the triangle of the rafters, which could only be reached by clambering across the roof, up rusty fire escapes and in through a roof light. The 'ensuite' bathroom was contained in a wooden box on the adjacent square of flat roof.

Conrad and David are both natural decorators and instantly saw the potential beyond the peculiarity. Conrad works as a media strategy consultant and David is a fine artist, but since meeting they have discovered a mutual passion for interior design and have started to work on other projects. 'David has an extraordinary eye for colour,' enthuses Conrad. Certainly, he has used it here in a particularly inventive and effective way, to delineate and rationalize architectural quirks, and to create drama in the two small bedrooms, neither of which is squeezed under the rafters.

LEFT *The smaller of the two bedrooms is lined with new panelling made from MDF and painted in 'Railings', an almost-black like the soft, velvety black of charcoal. The room doubles as a study and library with shelves lining the wall opposite the bed, and the effect of the dark panelling is to give the space an enclosed, secret feel. The floorboards are new oak treated with a dark stain.*

RIGHT *The end wall of the main room was always planned as a background for Conrad and David's collection of monochrome artwork, and this was one of the most important considerations when selecting its colour. Both of them love shades of grey and chose 'Chemise' as the dominant colour in this north-facing room, a grey that is soft and smoky but not cold. The chimney breast is painted in 'Hardwick White', a paler shade of grey that continues round the corner into the open-plan entrance hall.*

THIS PAGE *The hall of Jo Berryman's terraced house is in graphic monochrome, throwing into sharp relief the hot red stripe of stair carpet. Throughout the house she has painted the Victorian floorboards 'Cornforth White' and used 'Pointing' for doors, skirting boards and here for the stairs. Walls are 'Hardwick White' and it is interesting to see how the different shades of off-white work together, making 'Pointing' look brighter and 'Hardwick White' darker than they would in another context.*

LEFT *The wall behind the kitchen units is 'Dauphin', a colour based on an 18th-century earth pigment, here looking as chic and contemporary as a Stella McCartney suit. Highlights of red – in this room the lacquered kitchen chairs, the gingham tablecloth and the numbered storage jars – continue a theme that begins in the entrance hall. This is a clever combination of a rich colour that advances towards the eye, against backgrounds of receding neutrals.*

BELOW *The kitchen is incredibly light, thanks to the double-height glass extension at the back of the house, and opens into the more enclosed, intimate space of the family room with its traditional arrangement of a sofa and chairs around a fireplace. Walls and ceiling are in 'Pointing' and more warm reds are introduced in the rug and the vase of roses. Dolly makes herself comfortable on an armchair.*

PRETTY CHIC

Fans of Farrow & Ball come in all shapes and sizes – Jo Berryman is a particularly glamorous version. Young, extremely pretty and formerly married to the bassist of a super group, she has worked her way through fashion styling on magazines, followed by running a fashion boutique in Marylebone, to a career in interior design. She is currently working on the interior of a hip London teashop in collaboration with designer Danielle Proud and on the decoration of a folly in Gloucestershire.

'It's been an organic progression,' she muses. 'I still love fashion, although I did become a bit disaffected. Interior design is so much more durable and seems to tap into something instinctual. I see it in my three-year-old daughter Nico who is always making little pockets of space for herself. I guess what I am doing is the grown-up equivalent of creating a den under the table.'

Jo's North London den is both playful and sophisticated; a Victorian terraced house with fancy cornices, panelled doors and marble fireplaces, brought up to date with the addition of a two-storey glass extension and the subtraction of internal walls, giving the ground and lower ground floors an open-plan airiness and informality. Popping with colour and bathed in light, furnishings are a mix of retro and classic, traditional and unexpected. Linking all the spaces are floorboards painted in 'Cornforth White' and woodwork in 'Pointing'.

'I have always used Farrow & Ball paints,' says Jo. 'I am drawn to the absurd names and the colours have a muted quality that really seems to flatter the architecture of a house. I am quite visionary when it comes to choosing colour. I knew for example that the pillar-box red stair carpet would look amazing with the 'Hardwick White' walls. And I don't mind experimenting – let's try a bit of 'Dead Salmon' – it's such fun and you can always paint over it.'

Jo has recently discovered Farrow & Ball wallpapers. 'As soon as I saw "Bamboo" I thought, "this is going to be one of those iconic designs that will last forever". It reminds me of my childhood in Hong Kong, but also fits antiques and that eclectic, slightly eccentric British style of interior design I love.' She has used it in two different rooms to strikingly different effect. At the far end of the hall with its graphic monochrome paintwork, it lines a 'womb-like' study area where it matches the shelving painted in glossy 'Rectory Red' and echoes the red stair carpet, pulling the eye down the hall as soon as you step over the threshold.

ABOVE *The monochrome colour scheme of the entrance hall continues up two flights of stairs, feminized on the way up by a pretty 18th-century French-style chair and a needlepoint cushion embroidered with flowers. The scarlet stair carpet is confined to the stairs themselves, leaving landings in plain 'Cornforth White', giving emphasis to the red and white stripe of carpet and floorboards.*

LEFT *Opening off the hall is a more formal double sitting room, originally two receptions rooms each with its own marble fireplace, now knocked into one. A desk sits against what was once the back wall of the house, overlooking the kitchen, which is accommodated in a double-height glass extension. 'Cornforth White' floorboards and walls in 'Pointing' provide a quiet backdrop to a vibrant colour scheme of blue and yellow.*

RIGHT *At the top of the house, this spare bedroom is a glamorous boudoir. Its sophisticated furnishings include a modern four-poster bed, an antique bergere upholstered in a muted damask, an Edwardian mirror and a zebra-skin rug, set off by walls in elegant 'French Gray'.*

'Bamboo' appears again on the first floor, in a completely different guise. This floor, once three separate rooms, has been opened into a single space to make Jo's open-plan bedroom, bathroom and walk-in dressing room, with an elegant boat-shaped metal bathtub placed centre stage in the window of what was the front room, the bed next to the window overlooking the garden at the back and the dressing room round the corner again at the front. Walls are 'Card Room Green', a restrained, refined shade. 'You can see wonderful sunrises from this room and I love the way the colour of the walls changes with the light and with the seasons,' Jo enthuses. 'It has real warmth and almost seems to pulsate. A little while

RIGHT *The first floor is Jo's private domain, opened into a single space from front to back of the house to make a large bedroom with a bath at one end and a bed at the other. Walls are 'Card Room Green' and recently Jo gave the room 'a lift' by papering one wall in 'Bamboo'.*

ago, I decided that the room needed a bit of a lift, so I wallpapered the wall above the bed with more of my favourite "Bamboo", this time in neutral shades of honey. The bedhead is upholstered in a jacquard leopard print from Savoir Beds and the combination is a little bit suburban bordello!' she giggles. 'But it adds to that sense of luxury and to the comfort and coziness that is very important to me.'

Probably the coziest room of all is the ground floor family room that leads off the kitchen. Here, a buttoned Chesterfield sofa upholstered in grey velvet and two buttoned armchairs, one frequently occupied by Dolly, family dog and expert burglar deterrent, are gathered on a rug around the fireplace. Jo likes to describe her home as 'a museum of the self' and says that every week she 'curates a display' on this particular mantelpiece. 'Depending on the mood I'm in it might be positively brimming with objects, while at other times I might choose a single object for impact, perhaps a doll's head or a crystallized skull. But everything has a meaning for me. It's not just done for effect, it's eclectic with a purpose.'

LEFT *A freestanding bath sits in the bay window at the front of the house, privacy provided by shutters at night and an antique screen by day. A walk-in dressing room leads off the* *bathroom end of this girly retreat and the open fire adds to the feel of elegant luxury. As in other parts of the house, the floorboards are 'Cornforth White' and the woodwork 'Pointing'.*

ACCENTS OF ORANGE

Project Orange is a young, modern, award-winning architect and design team with bright, open-plan offices in a converted industrial building in Clerkenwell. No one sitting at the slick ranks of desks looks over the age of 40 and it is pleasantly counter-intuitive to learn that one of their favourite Christmas party games is a mark of devotion to Farrow & Ball paint.

LEFT *James Soane and Christopher Ash of Project Orange bought their flat on the first floor of a converted garment factory as a shell and divided the L-shaped space to leave a single large room that spans the building from front to back, with a kitchen at one end and a sitting area at the other. One long wall is painted in 'Railings' and the alcove is 'Lime White'.*

ABOVE *Walking through the windowless entrance hall, which has walls and ceilings also painted in 'Railings', into the main room has all the drama of emerging from a tunnel into the light. The variegated terracotta of the exposed brickwork on the opposite wall shadows the bursts of orange and red throughout the flat, such as the legs of the kitchen table seen on the left painted in 'Blazer'.*

'We have at least 150 Farrow & Ball paint charts lying around the office,' says James Soane, sitting at the kitchen table of the flat he shares with partner and business partner Christopher Ash. 'There are two versions of the game. In one we test our ability to identify particular shades by name, which is extremely difficult when it comes to all the different whites, and in the other we take turns to recite the name of a colour, sometimes having to invent one, which gets extra points if it goes unchallenged – "Oh yes, didn't you know, 'Grenadier Green'. It's one of their new ones." – that sort of thing.'

If further proof of devotion were needed, James can reel off a list of projects that feature Farrow & Ball: 'Chemise',

'Blazer', 'Stony Ground', 'Slipper Satin', 'Yellow Ground' and 'Etruscan Red' for a reconfigured 1980s house in Bloomsbury; 'Railings' for the façade of buildings in Whitecross Street, East London where their combination of renovation and new-build won a prize at The Design Awards in 2009; 'Arsenic' and 'Off-Black' for the Plus Seven Hotel in St Petersburg; 'All White' and 'Down Pipe' in Eynsham Hall hotel, a mock-Jacobean mansion in Oxfordshire. 'It's never difficult to persuade clients to choose Farrow & Ball over a less expensive paint. All you have to do is paint two sample areas, one with Farrow & Ball, another with a matching colour, and they will always choose the Farrow & Ball. It has a depth unlike any other paint.'

LEFT *Instead of attempting to brighten the entrance hall, which has very little natural light, James and Christopher have created visual drama with ceiling lights that make the wood floor glow and paintwork that looks almost black and seems to expand the sense of space. In fact, 'Railings' is a dark bronze colour and less harsh than a pure black. The low shelf is the protruding back of a plan chest, the drawers of which open into the study on the other side of the wall.*

RIGHT *At the sitting end of the main room, light pours in from a large metal window. 'People think that dark grey will suck up all the light,' says James Soane, 'but in this big room it actually seems to reflect it. It also works incredibly well with hot colours, which have all the more impact seen against it.' Here, the impact comes from the physalis lanterns, the patriotic cushion and the haloes of orange in the photograph of the London Docklands by night.*

LEFT *The bathroom is an internal room painted in 'Powder Blue', an archive colour, and the room is further brightened by the mirrored doors of a made-to-measure wall cabinet. Brick laid white tiles give the room a feel of old-fashioned solidity.*

RIGHT *The bedroom is lit by large, metal-framed windows and is painted bright 'Lime White'. The same accents of red, the bedhead painted in 'Blazer', the upholstery of the reproduction Mackintosh chair and the bedspread by Kvadrat, are more cheerful than sultry against a pale as opposed to a grey dark background.*

A more personal project was the re-decoration of James and Christopher's flat in a 1910 building near their offices. The handsome carved stone entrance flanked by expanses of glazed brickwork once opened into a garment-making factory. 'When they took up the floors during the conversion, they found thousands of pins and scraps of cotton under the boards,' says James. 'We bought the flat as a shell in the early 1990s when the idea of converting industrial buildings for domestic use was still quite radical. Obviously it helped that we are both architects.'

The space that James and Christopher bought was an L-shaped segment with three large, metal-framed windows and double doors onto a fire escape along the bottom edge of the L and a single, large window across its top. They lowered the ceiling height of the shorter leg so as to hide pipes and used its three windows to light a bedroom and adjacent study. Opposite are a bathroom and utility room, both without windows. The space that remained was a long room spanning the building, from the window and doors onto the fire escape on one side to the single window on the other. One end became the kitchen, the fire escape with its wide metal stairs and landing their 'sneaky back garden' with plants flourishing in large pots. The middle of the room is the dining area and at the far end, gathered in the light from the other window, is the sitting area.

The back wall of this long, multi-purpose room is bare brickwork and, until recently, the rest was painted 'Lime White'. 'We're a bit more sophisticated and grown-up than when we first bought this place,' smiles James, 'and we decided it was time for some colour'. The colour they chose was 'Railings', 'a typical architect's colour,' says James. 'We wanted to prove that such a dark shade doesn't need to be like some gothic nightmare and doesn't kill the light.'

This warm, moody charcoal covers walls and ceilings in the hall, making a theatrical prologue to the volume of the main room where the same colour almost seems to reflect rather than absorb light. It also throws into relief the splashes of red and orange that punctuate a mainly neutral scheme; whether the bright lanterns of physalis in a vase, or the upholstery of an Eames chair. James insists that these accents of orange are not an intentional visual pun, although he admits that 'people do tend to give us orange things'. But the bedhead and the legs of the kitchen table are painted in 'Blazer', which is the closest the Farrow & Ball chart comes to orange. Perhaps someone in his office could christen a new Farrow & Ball colour. 'Seventies Kitchen' anyone?

MODERN COUNTRY

Escaping from the city, from the crush of cars and the press of other people, can feel like taking

a deep breath of cool, calm air. For one family in this chapter, their expanded seaside cottage

is the setting for long summer holidays, for another, an elegant manor house is a weekend refuge

close to London but completely secluded; and for the last of the three, a village farmhouse

is the base from which one of its members travels the world as a fashion stylist.

THIS PAGE *In the large L-shaped hall from which rises a pretty 18th-century staircase, Karen Harrison has painted the walls 'Strong White', a neutral off-white that looks bright and clean when used with dark colours. Here it contrasts with the lead grey of 'Down Pipe'.*

SET PIECE

Karen Harrison, her husband Mark and their two children, Harvey and Rae, live in a Sussex village so perfectly pretty it might have been designed as a set for any number of gentle, period dramas. 'As soon as we found the place, I knew I wanted to live here,' she says. The old-fashioned feel is largely due to the fact that the whole village still belongs to an estate and all the houses are rented, rather than individually owned. Having already tried and failed to buy in the area, Karen and her husband Mark put their names on a waiting list.

LEFT *Karen has an unerring eye for a bargain, and even the kitchen Aga was bought second hand from a local company that specializes in refurbishing them. However, although the house is rented, Karen has insisted on using Farrow & Ball paint throughout because she loves its quality, here seen in 'Strong White' on the walls and 'Cornforth White' on the woodwork.*

ABOVE *Karen has stripped old floorboards back to the pale wood downstairs and replaced floorboards upstairs where she has painted them. The front door and its architrave and fanlight are painted in 'Down Pipe'.*

The first suitable house that became available was a farmhouse opposite the church at the end of the village where the fields begin and the Downs start to rise. The house is mainly 18th century, although parts of it date back much further, and in the middle of the last century a particularly successful farmer added a billiard room. More recently the house has been divided into two. The result is an interior with an unusual layout, Karen and Mark's portion having more space downstairs than up, including the large, L-shaped staircase hall.

Initially, Karen was dismayed by what she calls the internal 'muddle'. 'It wasn't helped by the decoration, which hadn't been touched for years. The whole place was in shades of yellow, with orange pine floorboards downstairs and stained blue carpet upstairs. But the individual rooms were potentially lovely and I realized it just needed knitting together.'

Karen was already a fan of Farrow & Ball paints, having used them throughout her London house. 'That was a typical terraced Victorian house in Queen's Park and we painted every room a different colour, some very strong, like "Carriage Green", which we used in our bedroom. But I realized that this house needed a completely different approach. The decoration had two roles: I wanted it to unify the house, but I also wanted to create a light, pale background; a blank canvas, as I was planning to rent out the house to be used as a location for magazine shoots. We also had to consider the fact that we didn't own the house, so we had to be careful not to over-invest.'

Karen knows what she is talking about when it comes to colour and light, having worked with photographers for the past 25 years as a fashion stylist. Although she studied at agricultural college and wanted to be a farmer, her passion for clothes took over after college when she got temporary work delivering mail around the building at IPC and applied for a job in the fashion department of *Woman's Own*. Since then, she has worked for everyone from Italian *Vogue* to Boden and still travels all over the world. 'In fact,' she says, making a surprising analogy, 'being a fashion stylist is a bit like being a farmer. You are often working outside and forever lugging heavy bags around. You have to be pretty fit.' Meanwhile, Mark lives the rural dream, working as a gardener for the nearby estate and looking after the children and Stanley the dog while Karen is away.

Paint has transformed the interior into a series of bright, interrelated spaces. Karen has used 'Strong White' for the walls in the kitchen, living room and all the hallways, and on the new upstairs floorboards. Helping to link them is the way the woodwork in the hallways, including the skirtings and door surrounds, are painted in 'Down Pipe', a warm grey, which traces and outlines these architectural features like the thick strokes of a black lead pencil. This back-to-front use of colour, instead of the more usual dark walls with white

LEFT *The house is rented out for fashion shoots, so Karen wanted to ensure a plain, pale background as a 'blank canvas' for photography. In the less formal of the two sitting rooms, the walls are 'Strong White' and the woodwork 'Cornforth White'. Curtains are in a slubby silk left over from the costumes used in a feature film, and the 1960s white PVC chair and oil painting were both bought in nearby Lewes where there is a weekly antiques market.*

RIGHT *In the same room, Karen doctored the 'horrible' reproduction fireplace by taking off the applied plaster decoration and knocking out the enclosed grate. The surround is painted 'Cornforth White' to match the rest of the woodwork and the radiator is in the same shade in an eggshell finish, 'The next best thing,' Karen says, 'to replacing it with something better looking.'*

LEFT *The cupboards in the main bedroom were 'ugly' until a carpenter friend of Karen's added the panelling and removed the handles in favour of push catches. A coat of 'Hardwick White' and the transformation was complete. Floorboards are new and painted in two coats of 'Strong White' floor paint. Walls are 'Cornforth White', the same colour as some of the woodwork downstairs.*

RIGHT *In the same room, the curtains are in unbleached artist's canvas from Whaleys of Bradford and the painted chest of drawers was a present. The mirror-framed 1930s print was bought from local antiques dealer Christine Loveland, a friend and the source of many of Karen's favourite pieces.*

BELOW RIGHT *The plaster on the bathroom walls was crumbling, but instead of stripping it off and re-plastering, Karen put up fake matchboarding made from scored sheets of MDF and painted in 'Pigeon' in dead flat oil.*

woodwork, is an idea Karen picked up in Sweden, as is her favoured palette of soft greys and smoky greens.

Karen has relied on paint for many of the effects in the house, using it on floors, stairs, furniture and to hide ugly radiators. 'You can transform a piece of furniture with a few coats of paint,' she says, citing the dining table painted in 'Cornforth White' to match the walls. Other cost-conscious tricks include covering the crumbling plaster of the bathroom walls in MDF, scored to look like matchboarding, then painted with her favourite flat oil finish in 'Pigeon', and using artist's canvas for curtains.

Furnishings are a mix of carefully chosen high street buys and antiques picked up from fairs. Even the Aga was a bargain, bought second hand from a firm that specializes in refurbishing them. 'Pretty much the only thing that wasn't cheap was the paint,' Karen laughs, 'but I think its quality shines through.'

LEFT *Sophie Conran was fortunate to move into a house already painted in a palette of off-white Farrow & Ball colours, which she says she would probably have chosen herself. The large kitchen-dining room is an extension at the back of the formal, double-fronted Georgian house. The walls are painted in 'Clunch', which is particularly appropriate in an area of the country where the chalky stone it takes its name from is so prevalent.*

RIGHT *Opposite the Aga, the dresser holds Sophie's collection of cookery books. Pink tulips pick up the pink of the sofa, adding another splash of brightness.*

CONRAN COUNTRY

When Sophie Conran comes up with a wishlist for her ideal country house, you can expect it to be unusually discerning. Belonging to a family for whom good design is quite literally part of the furniture, she has always lived in beautiful houses and says she spent her childhood flitting between her father Terence Conran's design studio and her mother Caroline's kitchen.

She and all her siblings are deeply involved in design and her surname is attached to all manner of stylish things and places, from shops and cafés to furniture and fashion. Lovely houses are a common currency; her brother Jasper must already have owned at least three of the loveliest country houses in England.

Sophie's first wish was for a good location; the house had to be within easy reach of London where she lives during the week and close to the school where both her children board. Fortunately, a particularly beautiful part of Sussex fitted the bill. 'One of my great friends lives

in this area,' explains Sophie, 'and I asked her to keep her eyes peeled. I knew it would be difficult to get exactly what I wanted, especially as so many of the houses around here are cottages, with low beams and small windows, which I find quite claustrophobic.' So, the list included high ceilings, good proportions, big windows, shutters and an Aga.

To Sophie's surprise, she didn't have too long to wait before her friend phoned and said she had found the perfect place for her. The house was for rent, not for sale, but Sophie decided she wanted it even before she saw it. Her only prerequisite was that the kitchen should have an Aga. Which it did. And not

only did she get her shutters and her high ceilings, she also got that rare thing: a house that combines grandeur with coziness and that is big enough for a family without endless rooms to spare. The setting of the house is another fabulous bonus. Located on the edge of a tiny hamlet, it is surrounded by gently undulating fields, but with the dramatic swoop of the downs serving as a perfect, bucolic backdrop.

From the front, the house is upright, symmetrical and classical, with particularly tall sash windows and a towering front door to match. A wide entrance hall houses the original wooden staircase, which winds up to the first and second

FAR LEFT *At the front of the house are two formal reception rooms, this panelled dining room and a drawing room on the other side of the staircase hall. This is the only room Sophie has re-painted, changing it from a green, which she felt made the room too dark, to 'Strong White', which has just the right slightly weathered feel to complement the 18th-century woodwork.*

LEFT *On either side of the dining room fireplace are original alcoves that Sophie uses to display glass. The skirting boards, fire surround and shutters are in 'Elephant's Breath', a very pale grey that sets off the greens and yellows that Sophie has introduced in fabrics and furnishings.*

BELOW *The family sitting room that opens off the kitchen is in the original mid-17th century part of the house, its ceiling opened up into the roof. Walls are painted 'Lime White' and furnishings make a contrast in plain, bold colours.*

LEFT *The elegantly elongated architecture of the house is particularly apparent in the first floor bedroom, where two tall windows in the façade of the house are echoed by equally tall but narrow windows on either side of the chimney breast. There is no need for curtains with a full set of working shutters and the effect of the plain panelling painted in 'Great White' has an elegant, classical simplicity reminiscent of Swedish Gustavian interiors. The fire surround is picked out in 'Lamp Room Gray'.*

RIGHT *Into the slightly austere architecture of the bedroom, Sophie has introduced a chintz-hung extravaganza of a bed, copied by her friend, set designer Sarah Neighbour, from a picture in a magazine. The chintz is from Brunschwig & Fils and is stylishly lined with a bright shade of turquoise.*

floors. On either side of this gracious centrepiece are two lofty reception rooms, a panelled dining room to the left and a drawing room to the right. On the floor above are two similarly large bedrooms, with accompanying bathrooms. But this is as far as the grandeur goes. Built in the mid-18th century, the front of the house is only one room deep. It extends at the back, but the proportions of the house change. The kitchen has a lower ceiling; adjoining it, the family sitting room has the beams, casement windows and inglenook of a cottage, and dates from the mid-17th century. Fortunately for Sophie, this early part of the house is single storey and its ceiling has been opened to the roof, so the beams are not of the type to make one feel claustrophobic.

The house came with a few pieces of furniture, but after only six months Sophie has already made it her own with antiques and paintings that she bought specially to suit the period of the rooms. A few pieces have been culled from her house in London, and some are family loans, including the pink padded footstools in the drawing room and the mahogany Georgian sideboard in the dining room – both overspill from her brother Jasper's houses.

The house also came ready decorated in a range of Farrow & Ball shades of white, which Sophie says are much the same colours as she would have chosen herself. So much so that the only room she has re-painted is the dining room, which she has lightened from a Farrow & Ball green to a Farrow & Ball white, while leaving the soft grey of 'Old White' that had been used for the woodwork of the window embrasures and is now complemented by yellow linen window seat cushions.

One of Sophie's most theatrical additions to the interior is her architectural, 18th-century-style four-poster bed, which she commissioned from a friend who is a set designer. In the dining room below she has placed antique gilt mirrors above the fireplace and mirrored sconces on the walls, so that when the room is lit by candles it is filled with the glitter of soft, reflected light. Counterbalancing this elegance and formality is a feeling of comfort; big cushions on deep sofas and the glow of a wood-burning stove. Sophie Conran quotes Dr Johnson on the home page of her website: 'To be happy at home is the ultimate result of all ambition.' And it just so happens that the date of the quote, 1750, matches the date of Sophie's new house. Ambition fulfilled.

ABOVE *The beamed entrance hall retains the low-ceilinged proportions of the original cottage, but has been updated with glazing and new wood floors. The house is a symphony of different shades of white; here, 'Lime White' walls and 'Old White' woodwork.*

The approach to Joanna Vestey's house on the north Cornwall coast is comprehensively rural. A-roads shrink to B-roads, a farm lane to a bumpy track. Without detailed instructions you wouldn't find it, but you know you have arrived when you cross a narrow bridge with rustic wooden rails and see a helicopter parked on the lawn.

TAKING A VIEW

The house is less swanky than the transport – a seaside cottage with pointed gables and clapboard walls. When Joanna and her husband Steve Boultbee Brooks bought the property four years ago, its principal attraction was the location. Tucked into sloping land surrounded by fields, it is far enough from the coast to be peaceful on a hot summer Bank Holiday, but close enough to have a view encompassing one of Cornwall's most popular bays. Even through a mist of drizzle, the glint of the sea spreading against the horizon is uplifting.

'In fact, you could hardly see the sea from inside the house when we bought it,' says Joanna, who is sitting on the sofa in the downstairs living room making a fireman out of plasticine for her six-year-old son Jago. 'The house was originally built as the count house for a lead mine and was much smaller,' she explains. 'Part of our plan to extend it was to gain views as well as more and bigger rooms.'

Behind the clapboard and under the gables, the old count house now swells into wide open spaces and double-height ceilings. At the centre of the house is the kitchen. The generous working area with its massive central island shelters under a ceiling at a height appropriate for a cottage, but opens into a dining area and staircase where the walls soar up to the roof. At the top of the stairs is a living area big enough to accommodate Jago's

THIS PAGE AND LEFT *The low-ceilinged area of the vast kitchen and dining room is the only part of the room that is not an extension. To the right of the dining table are stairs leading up to a large living area. The kitchen itself was designed by Plain English in stripped-back country style. The floor and skirtings are in 'Hardwick White'; the walls are 'Slipper Satin'.*

Scalextric, plus sofas, armchairs, a desk and beanbags made from recycled sailcloth. Three sets of French doors frame a panorama of sea and coast, and a decking balcony beyond them becomes part of the room on a warm day.

The whole house is incredibly light thanks to new windows and glass doors and the layout of rooms that lead one into the other and out again. 'We did exactly the same in our London house,' says Joanna. 'We opened it up so that the children could bicycle or run round.' Light flows between rooms through open doors and in the children's room through internal and external windows. This is enhanced by the pale colours used for the walls and furnishings.

The first impression is that everything is painted white. But Joanna is a photographer and very conscious of the effects of light and colour, and has done something more subtle. Look more carefully and you will see that she has used no less than ten different shades of Farrow & Ball white paint on walls, stairs, woodwork and floors.

Steve, a property investor also described in *The Sunday Times* Rich List as 'a polar explorer', has come

ABOVE *Stairs from the kitchen lead up to the space they call 'the estuary room' in honour of its panoramic views, which can be enhanced by use of the telescope. Until the cottage was extended, the sea could only be seen from the garden. Joanna has chosen a range of different off-whites, here 'Joa's White' for walls and 'Slipper Satin' for woodwork, knowing that bright whites would have been too dazzling in a house that is flooded with sunlight even on a grey winter's day.*

RIGHT *The downstairs living room leads into the kitchen and retains the beams and fireplace of the original cottage. Against 'Lime White' walls and in a predominantly neutral colour scheme, the warm browns of wood and leather acquire an added richness.*

THIS PAGE *Joanna chose creamy 'White Tie' for the main bathroom, and 'Cornforth White' for the skirting boards and floor. The outside of the bath is 'Pelt', a very dark purple that looks almost black against the pure white of the bath enamel. The new architecture of the house has an appropriately nautical feel, here introduced by the circular porthole window, designed to give bathers a soothing view of trees.*

BELOW RIGHT *Decking balconies are one of the many ways in which the design of the house makes the best of its views. 'Slipper Satin' applied to the walls of other rooms is used here for the woodwork and skirtings, while 'Stony Ground', one of the darkest whites in the house, covers the walls.*

RIGHT *Two circular windows in the children's bedroom overlook the dining area of the kitchen, an irresistible invitation to spy on grown-up dinner parties. The window surrounds and shutters are painted in 'Off-White', their shape echoed by the giant coloured spots of the rug. Walls are 'Slipper Satin'. The strong, bright colours of the rug, window blind, pictures and toys look fresh and jolly in a room where walls, floor and furnishings are all in shades of white.*

to join Joanna on the sofa and is making a plasticine duck for their three-year-old daughter Chloe. 'I always defer to my colour consultant,' he quips, smiling at his wife. 'She's got a great eye. And we both love Farrow & Ball. We used it in our London house and I must tell you a story about that. We asked our builder to paint a room a particular colour while we were away – it was a shade of white, I can't remember which. When we came back we walked in and didn't like it. But then we found the tin.' He roars with laughter. 'It turned out they had colour matched the paint using a cheaper brand. It was the same colour, but the effect was completely different.'

Joanna and Steve are both adventurers. When they first met, Steve was planning a trip from America to Russia across the Bering Strait in a vehicle Joanna memorably described as 'part Thunderbird, part combine harvester'. Drawn in by Steve's extraordinary energy and enthusiasm, Joanna took on the role of official photographer for the trip. It was also Steve who inspired her book *Faces of Exploration* for which she photographed 50 explorers. And it was when working on this that she first had the idea of finding a second home in Cornwall. 'I was visiting an explorer who lived in Bodmin, and I realized how much I love the coast here. It seemed like a mythical place and somewhere we could pile down to from London, where we could surf and relax, and have family and friends to stay.' Which is exactly what they do every other weekend and for weeks at a time in the holidays. Of course, it helps to commute by helicopter. 'It only takes an hour and a half,' Steve grins. 'But we really should paint the helicopter in a Farrow & Ball paint!'

COUNTRY HOUSE

As the preceding pages make abundantly clear, Farrow & Ball paints and wallpapers are as versatile as their admirers are diverse. Although the English country house was once regarded their natural habitat, their inimitable colours now adorn contemporary architecture and urban lofts as effectively as they do period panelling and old lime plaster. The country houses in this chapter are all beautified by Farrow & Ball, but even in this most traditional of contexts, the impressions created and the styles adopted are delightfully dissimilar.

THIS PAGE *The long inner hall is used as a dining room. Ben originally painted it 'Entrance Hall Pink', an archive colour that he has kept in the outer hall, but then decided that his collection of plaster casts looked more refined against pale grey and so re-painted it in 'Hardwick White' above the dado and 'Shaded White' below.*

RIGHT *The tiny kitchen opens straight off the drawing room and is inexpensively fitted with floor cupboards on three sides and wall cupboards opposite the window. Ben has prettified this utilitarian space with walls painted 'Ointment Pink', a selection of pictures and pieces of antique china including lustre and a Staffordshire cow.*

BELOW *Ben's apartment comprises one wing of this eccentric, contemporary country house. Three of his windows overlook the formal garden with its mini canals; the two on the right are his drawing room windows, the one on the left his kitchen window.*

IN PROPORTION

The pink, castellated façade of Bellamont House is a highway hazard. As you bowl along the Dorset lane from hamlet to tiny village, it suddenly appears between hedges; a sugary confection against grassy hillside, as bewitching as a glimpse of a unicorn. It is even prettier close up. Turning into the courtyard beneath arches topped with more crenellations is like entering a fairy castle. Here are gothic windows, white roses and exquisitely espaliered crab apples with fruit hanging like tiny lanterns.

This charming folly of a house was built some 15 years ago by former property developer Anthony Sykes and has all the architectural flourish of a stately home but without the inconvenience of scale. Despite the gate posts topped with curly-tailed hounds, the regal rooftop lion, the urns, the miniature cannon, the quatrefoils, medallions, pilasters and pediments, the house is the size of a comfortable parsonage. It isn't even one house. On either side of the two-storey central block are single-storey wings. One of these is a separate flat, built to house a grown-up daughter but now rented by architect Ben Pentreath.

Pink and pretty isn't Ben Pentreath's style. But classical is. And inside the pink casing, his slice of the house has nicely proportioned rooms with high ceilings and generous sash windows, spaces that he has furnished with characteristic elegance and restraint, and painted throughout with Farrow & Ball colours.

Ben Pentreath is a busy man. He is currently working on several housing projects in Cornwall and Devon, a classical terrace for Poundbury and a substantial country house in Oxfordshire, with a fistful of other new country houses in the pipeline. His eponymous Bloomsbury shop, which sells

covetable furnishings and accessories, including photographs by James Ravilious, resin lamps by Marianna Kennedy, plaster casts by Peter Hone and creamware crockery, has been credited with single-handedly revitalizing the area of Bloomsbury where he also lives and has his offices. And he has recently finished a project of meticulously measuring and drawing a series of fragile Georgian cornices from National Trust houses so that they can be accurately reproduced. As it happens, he is also about to move house and has just completed the decoration of his new rural abode in an adjacent village, again using paints from Farrow & Ball.

The combination of this, his most recent foray into interior décor, and the memory of how his current country flat looked before he got to work on it inspires a heartfelt exclamation, 'Ah, the power of paint!' Perched on the work surface of his tiny kitchen, which opens straight into the drawing room, he explains that the flat was 'quite a mess' when

ABOVE *Ben has painted the interior of this 18th-century bureau-bookcase in the drawing room vivid 'Chinese Blue'. This has the effect of throwing into pearly white relief the collection of plaster casts and fragments of antique coral that are artfully arranged on the shelves.*

RIGHT *Ben inherited the drawing room curtains, which filter the sunlight with much the same effect as the leaves on the other side of the window. He chose a neutral paint scheme of 'Bone' above the dado and 'Shaded White' below to act as a foil for furnishings in richer colours.*

THIS PAGE *There are two bedrooms opposite the drawing room and kitchen, both simply furnished with 18th-century mahogany and plain divan beds. Inexpensive Indian bedspreads in printed cotton, which Ben likens to Regency paisley, hang at the windows as makeshift curtains, and also cover the beds in both rooms. The walls in this room are painted in refined 'French Gray'.*

BELOW RIGHT *The second bedroom is smaller and more feminine, with patterned chintz upholstering the pair of 18th-century dining chairs and walls painted 'Light Blue' above the dado and 'Shaded White' below. Ben has deliberately confined himself to muted shades in this, his relaxed country retreat, but has enjoyed experimenting with stronger colours in his London flat.*

he took it on. 'I had stayed here as a guest when working at Poundbury, as Anthony's daughter Nina is a great friend. She and Joel have small children and they hadn't really bothered with the interior. When I heard that she was leaving I asked Anthony if I could take over and he agreed, and kindly offered to redecorate for me. But when he asked what colours I would like and I specified Farrow & Ball, he said I would have to pay extra because it is so expensive!' He bursts out laughing. 'You should definitely write that,' he says. 'Anthony won't mind a bit. And I didn't mind paying extra because it is absolutely worth it. You can try colour matching with cheaper brands of paint, but it's never as good.'

The colours Ben chose for the two bedrooms, drawing room and dining hall are calm, restful shades that hover between blue, white and stone. The pale terracotta of 'Entrance Hall Pink' warms the entrance hall and 'Ointment Pink' the kitchen. Pink is the colour that welcomes you through the front door into a space stacked with stuffed birds, gardening books, boots and coats. Just beyond is the wide, top-lit inner hall that doubles as a dining room. 'Originally I painted this the same pink,' Ben explains, 'but when I put up all the plaster casts it looked more pretty than architectural, so I changed it to "Hardwick White".' Kilims in rich tomato reds laid over coir matting radiate colour from the floor; but the rest of the room is in a refined palette of dark mahogany furniture, black and white engravings, creamware pottery and white plaster.

This same combination of a serene background enlivened by areas of bolder colour, red in particular, also characterizes the drawing room with more kilims covering floor cushions in front of the fire. Pale green curtains, which filter the light like sunshine through new leaves, add a frisson of acid to an otherwise mellow scheme. 'These paint colours are all ones I have used before,' says Ben. 'They are tried and trusted and, as far as I am concerned, totally reliable.' Which is why he has also used them in his London flat, his London offices and his London shop.

RIGHT *The small internal bathroom is lit from above and has walls painted in 'Bone', the same colour used in the drawing room. The faded tones of 18th-century coloured prints are shown to good advantage against this pale stone colour.*

ART HOUSE

Having a cake and not being able to eat it never did make sense. So it is always pleasing to find instances that prove the old adage wrong. Dermot and Tessa Coleman have several metaphorical cakes and are happily munching their way through them all: Dermot is a hedge fund manager, but is also studying George Eliot for a PhD; Tessa also worked in finance, but subsequently combined having four children with going to art school and being a successful painter. And their house combines architectural features from the medieval to the Victorian with the light, space and giant kitchen that are currently the ultimate desirable qualities for a family home.

This last advantage in life is particularly hard to come by. For obvious historical reasons, period houses tend not to have their kitchen in the biggest, nicest room. And if a house is listed and of architectural importance, it may be impossible to get planning permission to relocate the kitchen from a gloomy wing at the back to a sun-drenched reception room. This, however, is exactly what Dermot and Tessa have done and the result is an enviable updating of a venerable building.

Theirs is only the most recent in a series of modernizations, that have reconfigured the house since it was built in the mid-15th century.

FAR LEFT *The house is a patchwork of periods from medieval to Victorian. This wide, beamed gallery links the inner staircase hall with the kitchen and has a grand Tudor feel that is enhanced by the walls painted in deep, dark 'Bible Black'. The door at the end opens into the bright, voluminous space of the kitchen.*

ABOVE AND LEFT *The kitchen, dining and living room occupy the space that was once a double drawing room with tall windows and French doors leading into the garden. Walls are painted in 'Strong White', and the kitchen by Craigie Woodworks has an island painted in 'Skylight' and floor units in 'Pale Powder'.*

In the mid-17th century the great hall was divided into two storeys, a new staircase was installed and the main entrance was moved from the north to the south front. The next major change came in 1864 when the last rector to live here decided to return the house to its medieval origins and completely remodelled the façade in the gothic-revival style. Ceilings downstairs were raised to give the reception rooms more impressive proportions and various fragments of woodcarving were imported and incorporated, including part of a 17th-century rood screen that was taken from the church to make a suitably antique overmantel.

Dermot and Tessa have been far less cavalier, but they have completely changed the feel of the house by demoting the huge double room, which stretches from front to back of the house, from grand drawing room to kitchen, dining and living room combined. French doors open onto stone terracing where there are tables and chairs for alfresco meals, and the generous Victorian floor-to-ceiling windows look out over the garden with its wide lawns, mature trees and fields beyond. Simply but comfortably furnished with a specially commissioned table big enough to seat 20, two outsize sofas and contemporary paintings hung on expanses of white wall, the room is unrecognizable as the formal drawing room it once was.

The appropriation of the main reception room was possible because the house already has two large reception rooms on either side of the hall: one a library, the other a sitting room with a fat, velvet sofa and rich, red walls hung with a patchwork of paintings. And partly it was allowed because there was evidence that part of the drawing room was the original site of the 17th-century kitchen.

LEFT *By closing off the original front drive, Tessa and Dermot have relegated cars to the back of the house so that the front door now opens onto a formal garden of paving interspersed with flowerbeds. Walls and some woodwork are painted in 'White Tie'.*

RIGHT *Leading off the hall is this living room painted in vibrant 'Rectory Red', which combines with the dark floorboards, the heavily carved Victorian fireplace and the velvet upholstery for an effect of rich opulence. The colour was principally chosen as a background for some of their collection of paintings, including a watercolour by one of their sons.*

Although the kitchen is mainly white, colour has been used to great effect in other rooms: theatrical 'Bible Black' in the gallery that links the inner staircase hall with the kitchen, 'Rectory Red' in the living room and 'Chinese Blue', the intense shade of a summer sky at twilight, for an upstairs bathroom. 'Having so much space,' explains Dermot, 'gave us liberty to play with different moods. We don't like wallpaper, but we wanted interesting, sometimes unusual colours, variations across the whole range and a consistent finish. I love the way the paint both absorbs and reacts to different light.'

An important consideration was finding colours against which to display their large and growing collection of modern and 20th-century paintings. This is a shared passion, and though Dermot tends to buy from established artists while Tessa buys work from her teachers and peers, they enjoy each other's taste. 'Rectory Red' was chosen for

the sitting room because it is the shade of red that Ruskin thought best as a background for paintings. Here, next to a portrait of their eldest daughter by Hephzibah Rendle-Short, and beneath a watercolour by Gwen John, is a painting that hovers between the abstract and the figurative. 'That,' says Tessa smiling, 'is an original Gabriel Coleman.' It seems that at least one of their children has inherited the artistic gene.

ABOVE 'White Tie' is a linking neutral in a house where vistas from room to room and across halls and corridors offer tantalizing glimpses of strong colour, such as the 'Chinese Blue' seen here at one end of the first floor landing on the walls of the family bathroom.

LEFT The main bedroom, bathroom and dressing room lead one into another along the front façade of the house. Ruby red Victorian stained glass throws lozenges of rosy light onto the walls, which are painted in 'Parma Gray', a gentle shade more blue than grey, used and named by decorator John Fowler.

THIS PAGE *The walls in the main bedroom are also 'Parma Gray' and the red glow of the stained glass in the adjoining bathroom finds an echo in curtains in lustrous red silk. The combination of a pale, receding background colour with the warm, advancing red makes a visually satisfying contrast.*

A NEW TRADITION

Everyone knows what the archetypal English country house consists of. There is an Aga in a kitchen somewhere at the back; a musty boot room hung with damp Barbours; a 'snug' with a saggy sofa where the dogs sleep in front of the TV; and at the front of the house with the best views, a pretty drawing room that doesn't get used very often, as well as a cold dining room that gets used even less. But what if you could start from scratch? What if you could have an English country house, with all the charm and none of the inconvenience?

Interior designer Emma Sims-Hilditch has recently finished work on just such a house. When she began, there was nothing but a collection of ugly farm buildings on a West Country hill overlooking unspoiled countryside. Her clients were a couple she had known for 15 years and had already worked with. 'Their previous house was a 17th-century manor house in a village not far from here,' she says, 'and I had helped them, mostly with soft furnishings. When they told me their plans for the new house, it was the most exciting commission I could imagine.'

ABOVE *The 'snug' is also used as an informal dining and breakfast room. The shelving is painted 'Light Gray' with darker 'Mouse's Back' inside the shelving on which a selection of family photographs is displayed.*

LEFT *The house is perfectly arranged for modern living, with rooms in all the right places, including this 'snug' that opens off the kitchen. The quiet colour scheme of walls in 'String', ceiling in 'Pointing' and fitted cupboards in 'Light Gray' is echoed in the colours of the plain wool upholstery. The link room that leads through to the indoor pool can be seen through the door.*

BELOW *The kitchen is in shades of white: 'Slipper Satin' walls, 'Off-White' cupboards, except the island unit in 'Light Gray', and 'Pointing' for the ceiling. The Aga looks all the more impressive against these neutrals.*

ABOVE *To the right of the front door are a formal dining room and drawing room, both spanning the whole depth of the house with views to front and back. Double doors at either end provide vistas along the whole length of the house from*

the drawing room, seen here through the doors of the dining room, to the 'snug' and kitchen at the opposite end. Colours between rooms modulate rather than contrast, and are repeated and echoed in order to provide visual continuity.

ABOVE RIGHT *The dining room panelling is painted in 'Ball Green', gently dragged and with mouldings picked out by subtle lines of gilding. Looking across the dining table, the green makes a flattering background to a collection of 18th-century paintings on glass.*

BELOW *The drawing room has windows on three
sides affording spectacular views. Here again, the colour
scheme is predominantly pale and neutral with walls in
'Stony Ground', woodwork in 'Clunch', the ceiling in
'Pointing' and the cornice and decorative plasterwork
in 'Slipper Satin'. The strawberry red silk damask sofa
picks up the colour of the adjacent dining room curtains,
as does a red lampshade between the far windows.*

The brief was for a house that would combine 'the ease and luxury
of modern-day life within a traditional, classical setting'. The finished
product is spectacular both inside and out. Still looking as pristine as if
it had just been unwrapped from clouds of tissue paper, this updating
of a much-loved classic is Queen Anne in style and built in local stone
the colour of perfectly baked shortbread. Placed to make the most of its
king-of-the-castle position, the house is surrounded by newly landscaped
gardens with terraces, a stone gazebo and expanses of golden paving.

Adjoining the house is the modern equivalent of
the stable yard, an enclosed courtyard of garaging,
with staff accommodation above. And, linked to the
house by a glazed wing with a gabled roof, is a large,
glamorous indoor pool, with floor-to-ceiling glass
doors that slide away in summer and a slate floor to
the pool that rises up, sending water cascading into a
tank below, so that the space can be used for a party.

As well as glamour and whizzy technology, there
is panelling and a carved oak staircase, marble and
limestone fireplaces and an arrangement of rooms
that is almost open plan so that the drawing room
and dining room feel linked with the rest of the

LEFT *In this severely classical bathroom, the light stone of 'Savage Ground' used on the window seat doors and the bath panels makes an ideal complement to the large-scale black and white chequerboard of the floor. Walls are 'Off-White', cornice and ceiling 'Pointing' and the remaining woodwork is 'Slipper Satin'.*

BELOW *Bedrooms feature the Chelsea Textiles embroideries that are a favourite of the clients, here used for a quilted bedspread. 'Light Blue' walls pick up the colour of the embroidered flowers. The ceiling and cornice are in 'Pointing' and woodwork (not shown) is in 'Clunch'.*

house. A kitchen off the main hall opens into a 'snug' and there is a choice of spaces for formal or informal entertaining. You also get a laundry room, an airy boot room, a lift, a bathroom for every bedroom, an estate office and a handsome 'doggy room' beautifully fitted with cupboards, sinks and beds, specially designed to house two black Labradors in utmost canine comfort.

While the architect John Weir worked on the build, Emma and her client spent two years shopping. 'We went to see their house in South Africa, we went to Portugal to find furniture, to various spas to look at swimming pools and to London for inspiration and to find antiques.' It sounds like one, long, girly treat, but Emma is keen to emphasize that their choices were often surprisingly economical. 'My client is a huge fan of Chelsea Textiles, and we managed to re-use nearly all her curtains from the old house, adding a pelmet to ones that were too short,' she explains.

The recycled Chelsea Textiles curtains in 'Auricula and Roses' became the keynote for the colour scheme of the house. 'Those gorgeous raspberry pinks and greens were the colours we picked up for the drawing room and dining room,' says Emma, 'and we used greens and blues in the bedrooms.' Having made an initial selection of paints for each room, Emma consulted Joa Studholme, a leading Farrow & Ball colour consultant. 'Joa was so helpful,' she says. 'In most cases she agreed with our choices, but she gave some excellent advice and it was really good to have a second opinion on a project as big as this.'

The house uses a wide variety of Farrow & Ball colours, from darker shades such as 'Picture Gallery Red' in the wine cellar and 'Ball Green' in the dining room, to neutrals 'London Stone' in the swimming pool room and 'String' in the 'snug'. As a background for oil paintings and a foil for the rich fabrics of curtains and upholstery, the plain matt walls have just the right feel of understated quality. It looks so perfectly judged that it is a surprise to learn that the client initially specified wallpaper throughout the house. 'We were told we couldn't wallpaper for a year, until the plaster had settled,' Emma smiles. 'Now, I think the paint will stay.'

THIS PAGE *The spectacular indoor pool has a ceiling in 'Joa's White' and walls painted in 'London Stone', a neutral that matches the colour of the limestone flooring almost exactly. Glass doors beneath pillared porticoes slide away into the walls when the weather is warm enough and the floor of the pool can be raised to lie flush with the limestone, transforming the space into a summer ballroom.*

THIS PAGE *Part of a structural wall between the kitchen and the informal sitting room was removed to give an open-plan feel to this part of the house. The remaining central section of the wall is filled by a dresser painted 'London Stone'. The rest of the units are 'Off-White'. Walls and door are 'Savage Ground', one of Lulu Carter's favourite neutrals, while the ceiling is 'Slipper Satin'.*

PAPER PATTERN

Lulu Carter has nearly 30 years' experience in interior design and has been using Farrow & Ball paints for as long as she can remember. As a designer who avoids 'high fashion', she has always used wallpaper in her schemes, even through the relentlessly plain and neutral decades when pattern was effectively wiped clean by minimalism, so she was thrilled when her favourite paint manufacturer started to produce it. 'The fact that I already knew and liked Farrow & Ball paints and the pigments in them made their wallpapers an obvious choice,' she says. 'I often use them for projects, as they tend to give a lift, and in some cases real impact. Usually, a mix of painted walls and paper is the most pleasing.'

ABOVE LEFT *The house has two front doors, a result of a long history of additions and alterations. This door is situated in a Victorian porch, added at a quaint angle in Tudor style and leading round a corner to double doors and the staircase hall. The pale honey of the exterior stonework continues in the interior of the house, which is characterized by a palette of neutral sands, stones and pale greys.*

ABOVE *'Ringwold' wallpaper provides a welcome in the hallway and continuous, muted pattern on the stairs and landings, from which other rooms radiate. Woodwork is in 'Stony Ground' for the door and skirting boards, and 'Clunch' for the architrave, providing simple definition for these internal architectural features.*

A recent example of a Lulu Carter interior given lift and impact by Farrow & Ball is a pretty, period house in Lincolnshire. On the outskirts of the village next to the church, the house was once a chantry and parts of it date back to the Middle Ages. Later additions include Georgian sash windows and Victorian extensions that give the house a meandering feel. The interior, however, had been 'overdone' with inappropriately grand fireplaces and too many 'dinky little details'.

This is the fourth house that Lulu has decorated for this particular family over the years and she describes them as friends rather than clients. 'I know their style so well now,' she explains, 'that they were

ABOVE *'Ringwold' wallpaper continues up the stairs, matched with a carpet in a pale shade of sand. The warm browns of the antique desk and the 18th-century stair rail almost glow against this pale background of soothingly similar shades.*

LEFT *Fabrics in grass green, deep purple, and a combination of the two, look contemporary and inviting in the family sitting room that adjoins the kitchen. Walls are 'Savage Ground' and the ceiling is 'Slipper Satin' in a continuation of the decorative scheme in the kitchen, which helps to link the two spaces together.*

BELOW *A small motif is always pretty for an attic bedroom. 'Polka Square' is as plain and understated as a patterned wallpaper can be, adding gentle, unobtrusive interest and here matched with paintwork in 'Pointing'. The woollen bedspread picks up the same blue and magnifies it.*

RIGHT *A detail of the wallpaper in the same room shows how the texture of Farrow & Ball papers is key to their effect. Even a simple pattern like this has a three-dimensional quality that contributes to its handmade feel, as well as its visual impact. The wallpapers may look delicate, but they are easy to clean.*

able to give me a pretty free hand. They like a contemporary, clean, unfussy look, so the house needed stripping back completely in terms of decoration. We also rearranged some of the space, to make ensuite bathrooms and to open up the kitchen into the family room next door. They have dogs and teenage children, so the decoration had to be practical as well as good looking.'

Lulu's decision to use the large-scale leaf and sprig 'Ringwold' for the entrance porch, the inner hallway and the staircase provides a decorative core for the house, from which the downstairs reception rooms and kitchen with plain walls in coordinating colours radiate. 'I love this design in these pale but earthy colours,' Lulu enthuses, 'It tones so well with the new limestone flooring. The pattern is the perfect blend of the traditional and the contemporary, and it also has a nice country feel. As soon as the wallpaper went up, the space seemed fresher and lighter.'

Since moving from London in the 1990s, Lulu has gathered a growing crowd of clients in Lincolnshire and the adjacent counties, to add to her client base of more southerly customers. She is so busy that she often works at weekends and it is not unusual to have 15 different projects on the go at once. Current commissions include a house in the Cotswolds, another in Norfolk and redesigning a cloakroom and utility room in a 'major stately home'. 'I use Farrow & Ball wallpapers wherever I can,' she says, 'and have just finished a bedroom that I papered in the same "Ringwold" colourway used here. It looks stunning.'

THIS PAGE *A riveted metal Brunel bath from Aston Matthews takes centre stage in the main bathroom, its exterior painted in chic 'Dauphin'. Walls are 'String', the ceiling is 'Pointing' and the floor-to-ceiling sash window is 'Wimborne White'. The hardness of metal and stone is softened by lavish curtaining.*

COTTAGE

What is it that makes a house a cottage? Is it low beams, small rooms and a country setting,

or is it a mood as much as a location or an architectural style? The two houses on the following

pages couldn't be more different. One is deep in a remote, rural setting, the other is in the

heart of London. One has a kitchen the length of a tennis court, the other has tiny

rooms on several floors. Both are plainly cottages.

'When I first saw this house many moons ago, there were oil lamps glowing in the windows,' says Sandra Whitmore. 'The old lady who lived here had no electricity. Eventually she got a fridge, but she kept biscuits in it because she didn't appreciate what it was useful for.' Deep in a wooded common, as far 'off-road' as you are ever likely to find a house in the well-populated Home Counties, Sandra Whitmore's cottage retains all the romance of rural isolation, while having gained every modern convenience, including a handsome Smeg fridge.

ABOVE *The new kitchen extension has been clad in weatherboarding painted in 'Blue Gray', the same colour that the windows are painted both inside and out. This is one of the ways in which Sandra has blurred the distinction between the interior of the house and the garden.*

LEFT *The kitchen was built against the rear wall of the original cottage and more recently extended at this end where there is a door onto a terrace. The kitchen units by Plain English are 'Card Room Green'; the walls are 'Pointing'.*

BELOW *The ground floor of the cottage has been extended in all directions, including this entrance hall that has windows looking out over the surrounding garden. The walls are in 'Pointing' and the window frames in 'Blue Gray'.*

Love this.

ISOLATED CHARM

Ten years ago, when she and her husband John first moved here, Sandra gave up a long career as an art director in advertising to devote herself to painting. Her large, freely drawn canvasses are inspired by the nature that envelops her home and by the mudflats and seascapes that lap at the door of the cottage on the coast nearby, where they like to de-camp for winter.

The cottage on the common sits in the middle of its informal garden, some of which has clambered up its walls, as snug as a red brick chicken in a nest of greenery. There is a network of paths, some also made of brick, some of gravel, punctuated by clusters of stone sinks, pots and mossy staddle stones, and behind the house there are three small buildings, along with a barn. 'I love sheds,' says Sandra, which doesn't really do justice to the trio of sturdy little buildings. One is her studio, stacked with canvasses

ABOVE *Much of the colour in the cottage is courtesy of the textiles Sandra collects, such as these pieces draped over the arm of a settle in the entrance hall. The antique linen sacking is almost exactly the same shade of off-white as the 'Pointing' on the walls.*

RIGHT *The living room, which occupies the ground floor of the original cottage, would once have been divided into separate rooms. Between the dark oak beams the walls are painted in 'Pointing' and the windows are 'Castle Gray'.*

and work in progress, one is a utility room and one is John's office. The barn is for storage. 'As you get older I think you need more space,' Sandra muses. 'I hesitate to throw things away, even little pieces of paper – anything can be an inspiration – books, feathers, shells, minerals.'

Sandra has surrounded herself with artistic inspiration, both inside and out. Beyond the garden is a meadow that belongs to the cottage. 'The land has never been ploughed and it is a haven for unusual wild flowers and insects. The meadow attracted me more than the house.' Sandra loves insects and has based a series of paintings on her observations of them.

The boundaries between the informal garden and the surrounding common are blurred and there is the same blurring between the interior and exterior of the house. When the weather is warm, the four doors and any number of windows stand open, but even on colder days there is a strong sense that the outdoors has been welcomed inside. Garden

Love this

furniture is dotted around the living room and a garden table and chairs sit at one end of the kitchen where, just outside the back door, the arrangement is repeated on a paved terrace. The floor in the kitchen and living room is brick, as if the garden paths have walked inside, and today a big green glass vase holds branches of medlar and quince cut from the trees just beyond the window. Even the paint colour, 'Blue Gray', has been used both inside and out.

Natural forms provide sculptural decoration throughout the house. Sandra is a collector of many things, from antique steel scissors and Indian textiles, to minerals, shells and kitchen colanders. A copse of coral sprouts from the top of a chest in the living room and the serrated edges of giant clam shells are silhouetted on windowsills, while old stone and marble mortars of various sizes are heaped with smaller shells. On a sideboard, the vertebra of a whale looks more like a contemporary sculpture in wood than the remains of an animal. There are great stacks of magazines and columns of books, and folded piles of embroidered fabrics that Sandra buys on trips to India. There is so much stuff it ought to be chaotic, but her artist's eye has gathered and arranged it so that the effect is visual richness rather than muddle.

The kitchen is the biggest room in the house, built as a lean-to against the back wall of the original timber-framed building of two rooms downstairs and two above. The house has been extended in other directions, adding a smaller sitting room and a large entrance hall downstairs, with a bedroom and bathroom above it. The result is a rambling and surprisingly spacious interior, despite the diminutive proportions of the oldest part of the house.

Consistent paint colours help to tie the different periods of architecture together. 'Blue Gray' has been used for all the woodwork apart from the kitchen, which is 'Card Room Green', and 'Pointing' has been used for all the walls. Sandra has been known to use Farrow & Ball eggshell for her paintings on canvas and for their frames. 'I find the colours very peaceful,' she says. Which from someone who values rural isolation so highly is praise indeed.

ABOVE *Despite its sloping floors, head-grazing beams and general antique charm, the house is fully equipped with all modern conveniences, including sleek, contemporary bathrooms, in this case with a jacuzzi bath and walk-in shower. Sandra's favoured palette of pale greys and off-whites, which forms a peaceful backdrop to brighter colour in other rooms, reigns supreme here, with tiling a slightly darker shade than the 'Blue Gray' of the matchboarding and walls painted in 'Pointing'.*

LEFT AND RIGHT *A narrow, planked corridor leads to the main bedroom where the floorboards are painted in 'Blue Gray' and the walls again in 'Pointing'. The low-set window, like all the windows in the house, has no curtains to shut off the view of the garden and the common beyond. The patchwork quilt is antique.*

SMALL WONDER

Among the novels and biographies and books about art on Helen Ellery's bookshelves are children's books that anyone between the ages of 40 and 60 will remember with a rush of nostalgia. Some of her favourites are about Milly Molly Mandy, the little girl with a neat bob of dark hair and a stripey dress, who played with 'little friend Susan' and lived in a village in 'the nice white cottage with the thatched roof'. Opening her copy at random to an illustration of a bedroom in Milly Molly Mandy's house, furnished in impeccable 1950s cottage style, Helen laughs, 'These drawings were obviously a great influence on me – that bed is just like mine.'

Helen Ellery's tiny urban cottage is laced with nostalgia. The book on the table beside her old-fashioned wooden bed is *The Family From One End Street*, another children's classic, and there is a playful childlike feel to many of her design ideas: the fairy lights looped in the kitchen with shades made from the papery orange seed heads of physalis; the high, built-in bed in the downstairs bedroom like a bunk in a gypsy caravan; the Ordnance Survey maps of favourite places pasted onto the walls in the hall; and the floor-to-ceiling walls of blackboard paint where she has chalked drawings of a blue tit, a conker and a horse chestnut leaf, and labelled them as if for a lesson about nature.

Nature is Helen's main source of inspiration, but even nature is intermingled with nostalgia. She describes the design ethos of her interior design company I Love Home simply as 'to bring the outside

LEFT *The tiny front sitting room on the first floor above the shop manages to accommodate a sofa, an armchair and a wall of books to the left of the fireplace. Photographed in autumn, the house is dressed for the season with orange gourds, pumpkins and the seed heads of physalis glowing against the soft colours of paintwork, with 'Pigeon' on the walls and panelling and 'All White' on the fireplace and woodwork.*

ABOVE RIGHT *Helen's wire-haired Jack Russells, Bert and Mabel, stand guard at the door of the shop, the window of which is decorated in an autumnal theme.*

RIGHT *The kitchen opens onto a tiny roof terrace, crammed with pots and lush with flowers and vegetables. The neat floor and wall cupboards are painted 'Pigeon', a visual link with the adjoining sitting room, and the floorboards are in 'Skimming Stone'.*

inside' and says in the introduction to her book, which is entitled *Outside Inside*, 'my heart and mind are always yearning for the memory of my country upbringing'. She particularly loved the garden of her childhood with its vegetables and greenhouse, lawns and fruit trees. 'When I first arrived in London I had real difficulty adjusting. And that is why I had to make a sanctuary that reminded me of the country. Even now I find myself looking out for a sprig of grass that has pushed through the pavement and wanting it to survive. So many people seem locked in a world of mobile phones, earphones and computer screens, which prevents them from seeing, smelling and hearing what's around them.'

Helen's antidote to too much concrete and technology is to 'reconnect with the seasons'. And this is why the pictures on her blackboard walls are of conkers. 'Next month, it will be holly and robins,' she says, 'and the lights will be decked with berries instead of physalis, and there will be lots and lots of greenery. I will change the blinds and the bedspread, and put dried fruit in the oven so that the scent

ABOVE AND RIGHT *A deep sofa fills almost half the floor space in the sitting room. Helen says she yearns for the countryside when in London and many of her paintings are landscapes offering small windows onto hills and fields. Curtains in striped ticking take the place of doors, freeing up valuable wall space.*

BELOW *The kitchen table is tucked between the stairs and the sitting room in the space that was once the landing. Helen kept the section of panelled wall that divided the room, painted it 'Churlish Green' and hung it on the wall next to the table. The stairs are painted in 'Carriage Green'. Green is one of Helen's favourite colours.*

spreads through the house.' She even has a productive garden on the roof terrace outside her kitchen, currently bursting with 'relentless autumn tomatoes'.

Adapting your interior to the seasons is a very appealing idea, but Helen admits that it is made easier by the fact that her house is so small. The ground floor is her shop and office, the floor above her kitchen and living room, the third floor is her bedroom and bathroom, and all are little rooms. She is converting the basement for guests and extra storage, and has built an extension filling what was once the tiny back yard. Into this extension, above which is her roof terrace, she has squeezed a raised bunk that has cupboards beneath and next to it a diminutive bathroom.

Helen's previous house was a few doors away in this quiet Clerkenwell side street and she was already well practised in the art of shoehorning. Space-saving tricks include using curtains instead of doors between rooms and for cupboards, and the removal of a partition wall on the first floor allowing her kitchen to spill onto what was once the landing. She cleverly mixes big furniture, such as her deep-seated sofa and generous double bed, with more compact pieces, small side tables and light wooden chairs.

Farrow & Ball paints, with their natural ingredients and organic colours, suit Helen's design philosophy. She particularly likes green, and has used 'Carriage Green' for the stair treads, 'Churlish Green' for the panelled kitchen wall and 'Pigeon', which looks grey in some lights and green in others, for the kitchen joinery. The ground floor bedroom is 'Calamine' and, with light dropping down from the skylights, has the soft glow of the inside of a shell. 'The colours I have chosen all feel close to nature, so they are soothing and easy to live with,' she says, with the satisfaction of someone who has nearly finished feathering their nest.

ABOVE *An inner entrance hall leads from the shop to the stairs and the spare bedroom at the back. Helen has papered the walls and door with Ordnance Survey maps of places she knows and loves, from Ambleside to the Scilly Isles. Walls are 'Lamp Room Gray' and the floorboards are painted in 'Skimming Stone'.*

LEFT *An Edwardian oak bed, straight from the pages of Milly Molly Mandy, leaves space for little else in the top floor bedroom. A window cut through the original planked wall looks into the bathroom. The unattractive regulation fire door has been disguised under more Ordinance Survey maps and Helen's favourite landscape painting hangs above the bed against walls painted 'Pale Powder'.*

RIGHT *Helen has lined the walls of her ground floor office and shop with matchboarding painted 'Cornforth White' and incorporating alcoves for extra storage. The window display of twigs and physalis lanterns spills across the desk where Helen's book* Outside Inside *lies open. The colour green is a constant, but the changing seasons dictate how Helen dresses up her rooms, whether with spring flowers or winter berries.*

PART TWO

COLOURS

'Colour is everything, colour is vibration like music,' said Marc Chagall. 'Colour is the place where our brain and the universe meet,' declared Paul Klee. Interior designers tend to be less poetic. But we all know, whether through the depression brought on by a shade of hospital green or the delight of candlelit dining in a room where ruby red walls glow, that colour is powerful stuff. From chaste white to deepest purple, the following pages show how to use that power wisely.

ABOVE RIGHT *Double doors in this grand London house have panelling picked out with frames in 'Blackened' and central panels in 'All White'.*

BELOW *In the double-height dining area of Jo Vestey's kitchen, the floors and skirting boards are painted 'Hardwick White', a soft grey the colour of faded limewash that looks at its lightest here in a space bathed in daylight. Walls and stairs are 'Slipper Satin'.*

BELOW RIGHT *White mugs, white milk, a white enamel sink with a lovely view and a big sash window painted in 'Strong White', one of the brighter shades in the Farrow & Ball range of whites.*

FAR RIGHT *Karen Harrison has chosen two cool off-whites for her kitchen, 'Cornforth White' for the concrete floor and the skirtings, and 'Strong White' for the cupboards that hold the family's huge record collection.*

THE PALETTE

All White

Wimborne White

Pointing®

Strong White®

Clunch®

Slipper Satin®

Off-White

Joa's White®

Shaded White

Blackened®

ALL WHITE

The physics of light can seem magnificently counter-intuitive. For example, how can

it be that white light is composed of all the wavelengths of the electromagnetic spectrum,

in other words a blend of many colours? It seems so unlikely, since we see white as an absence

of colour; pure and unsullied, hence its powerful symbolism as clothing for the virginal. True

white is a rare thing and most of the whites we live with are tinted or tainted. Perhaps the

closest nature comes to absolute white is fresh snow, its tiny crystals reflecting the sky.

LEFT *The top floor of Alison Hill, Head of Design for Home for a major retailer, and her husband John Taylor's late 18th-century terraced house in South London is painted throughout in 'All White', the brightest of all the Farrow & Ball whites. The house has high ceilings and five floors including the basement, and these rooms feel as if they are floating among the treetops.*

BELOW *In the same bedroom a mirror reflects floor, ceiling and door, all in 'All White'. Simple furnishings have extra impact in a space that is as bright as a light box. Even wooden coat hangers take on a sculptural quality.*

White has a long history in interior design. Before the mid-18th century, it was the most commonly and widely used paint colour, usually in the form of limewash, coating everything from the lumpy, hairy plaster of a cottage wall to the decorative ceiling of a 16th-century mansion. As the background or scheme of a room, white has long flashed in and out of fashion. Some of Georgian architect Robert Adam's most famous rooms, such as the library at Kedleston Hall, use shades of white to create unity and dignity in combination with decorative intricacy. After the peacock brilliance of the Regency and the lugubrious twilight of the Victorian parlour, Arts and Crafts designers again sought the freshness and simplicity of white paint, a trend that continued to brighten interiors throughout the Edwardian period when there was also a craze for white-painted furnishings.

More recently, white has become the favoured non-colour of modernism, the inevitable gallery background for contemporary art, and the *sine qua non* of minimalism. Since it was first unveiled some

THIS PAGE *On the same floor of the same house is an office, again painted in 'All White', including the fitted cupboards. The palette is strictly monochrome and the decorative twigs in a vase on the floor are silhouetted like trees in a snowy landscape.*

80 years ago, decorator Syrie Maugham's iconic 'all white' drawing room at her house in Chelsea has spawned thousands of versions with the same long, low sofas and rugs in shades of cream, chic white walls and the enlivening glint of mirror and chrome.

White has been used so hard in the last century that it has become a decorating cliché, often resorted to as a blameless choice, a get-out-free card from the prison of the style police. At its worst, white can be bland, but as a deliberate and disciplined

THIS PAGE AND RIGHT
Architect William Smalley's flat is on the second floor of an 18th-century terraced house in Bloomsbury. His living room and bedroom retain their original panelling, fireplaces and shutters, all of which he has chosen to paint in bright 'All White' in dead flat oil, a suitably period finish. The effect, combined with sparse furnishings and minimal clutter, is calm and ordered. Floorboards have simply been scrubbed.

decorating decision, as opposed to a feeble, default position, white can also be unbeatably beautiful.

In some areas of life, brilliant white is still aspired to because of its association with cleanliness. Washing powders contain chemical brighteners to make our underwear, towels and t-shirts appear spotless, and all kinds of paper, from lavatory to printer, is bleached to provide us with the proverbial 'clean sheet'.

ABOVE RIGHT *In the same flat, a single piece of iconic modernist furniture, a chair by Marcel Breuer, placed on its own against white walls has the presence of an exhibit in an art gallery, although William insists it is as comfortable as it is handsome.*

RIGHT *Key to the serene effect is a lack of clutter. William has allowed himself two small bursts of paint colour inside storage cupboards on either side of the fireplace; this one is 'Light Blue'.*

'White goods' is shorthand for kitchen appliances, referring to their generic icy sheen with its connotations of germ-free hygiene. And, after a period of increasingly adventurous experimentation with every pastel shade from primrose yellow to avocado, bathroom suites have largely reverted to a pristine pallor.

Not so long ago, when gloss white woodwork and white emulsion ceilings were the common denominator of the domestic interior, brilliant white with its cold, chemical glint of blue was the leading paint shade. Professional decorators knew better and mixed their own, but for the rest of us, this was the white paint we took for granted, the only white we knew. And then there was a revolution. Farrow & Ball introduced its paint chart with a selection of whites. Here were whites the colour of Portland stone, silvery sand or top of the milk.

The first Farrow & Ball paint chart featured five variations on the theme. At number one on the chart was 'Lime White', a colour based on white limewash or soft distemper. Number two was 'Hound Lemon', 'Off-White' was the third colour and considered daringly grey, while 'Old White' at number 4 seemed daringly fawn. As for number 5, 'Hardwick White', surely this was not 'white' at all?

In the years since those early charts, the range of Farrow & Ball whites has become legendary. There are currently nearly 30 of them depending on where you draw the line, whites of every hue: soft, bright, misty, milky, faded, pearly, ivory, creamy. Seen against the dead

RIGHT *Sliding doors at one end of the ground floor living room in this central London house slide away to reveal a kitchen of space-age streamlining with cupboards in white lacquer and walls and ceiling painted in 'All White'. The contrast with the adjacent room with its rich upholstery and warm colours is theatrical, and the wall-mounted aquarium that glows blue and green has an ethereal luminosity in the midst of so much white space.*

LEFT *The magic of a white wall is the way it throws into relief whatever is placed against it, making shapes appear sharper and colours brighter, as in this simply furnished bedroom.*

THIS PAGE *Upholsterer and furniture designer Aiveen Daly describes herself as 'a slave to Farrow & Ball', which she has used throughout her house as a foil to brilliant colour. The hall walls are 'Strong White'. The floor and woodwork are 'Cornforth White'.*

white of icing sugar or a new plastic plug, these whites don't look white at all. But in the context of a room, whether an urban loft flooded with light or a panelled drawing room, they are shades that flatter and enrich. And, in contrast with dark, strong colours, they do indeed look 'white', even in the case of 'Hardwick White', a shade that looks far from white upon first glance at the Farrow & Ball colour chart.

Cleanest of all the Farrow & Ball whites is 'All White'. This relatively bright white is described as 'neutral' and is made using predominantly white pigment (titanium dioxide). Other whites may have more complex recipes such as 'Wimborne White', which is white with the addition of yellow oxide, 'Off-White', tinted by red oxide, black and bright yellow, and 'Great White', containing yellow oxide, black and violet.

Faced with this extraordinary array, the lazy side of the brain may experience a momentary nostalgia for the days when you bought a tin of any old white paint and hoped it would fade and mellow to a less antiseptic shade, courtesy of dust and nicotine. We are all familiar with the truisms about white paint; the fact that it reflects light; the way

ABOVE *Aiveen loves the contrast between muted and brilliant colours. Against a background of walls in 'Strong White' above dado level and 'Elephant's Breath' below, she has used darker neutrals for upholstery, curtains and rugs, with startling splashes of fuchsia pink provided by cushions and the vintage leather pouffe.*

LEFT *The dining room has the same paint colours as the living room and a floor painted in 'Cornforth White' with vintage furnishings in neutral tones. In this context of gentle colour, the red lampshade and flowers become focal points.*

THIS PAGE *The room behind architect Ben Pentreath's office on the first floor of a Georgian house in Bloomsbury is a staff kitchen and dining room. The Eero Saarinen table and Hans Wegner 'Wishbone' chairs are 20th-century design classics that look all the more fresh in this period setting of Georgian panelling and dentil cornice. Their pale wood and white lacquer are complemented by walls in 'Clunch' and ceiling in 'All White'.*

it opens up space; the clean, calm effect of a pure white wall. But the joy of having so many versions of white to choose from is the unlimited opportunity it offers for creating schemes that are not only clean and fresh but also soothing thanks to their infinitely subtle modulations.

A room painted a uniform shade of one of the brighter whites is a gleaming blank canvas. Paint the floor white too and the room becomes a light box. Against this background, a splash of any punchy colour has extra impact, especially if the rest of the furnishings are neutral or monochrome. A vase of pink tulips is extra pink, an apple green cushion shouts for attention, a vibrant painting almost jumps off the wall. In the same way, pieces of furniture take on a sculptural quality, their outlines silhouetted like the bare, dark branches of trees thrown into relief against a field of snow. This is the use of white that feels most contemporary, even in a period house, minimizing the architectural detail of a room to make it a seamless container for possessions, and expanding the sense of space.

Architect William Smalley, known for 'sensitive modernism', has painted the Georgian panelling and shutters, the window frames, doors and ceiling of his Bloomsbury flat in 'All White', such that only gentle shadow lines trace the three-dimensional quality of the beautiful woodwork. A more traditional approach, of which decorator John Fowler was an undoubted master, is to use differing whites in order to emphasize architectural detail. This can be as straightforward as painting the flat field of a panel a slightly darker shade than its surrounding frame or a door slightly darker than its architrave. The lighter colour advances and the darker colour recedes, tricking the eye into seeing an exaggerated perspective. Grand rooms with complicated schemes of woodwork and plasterwork to reflect the classical orders often look their best when the various elements of dado, panelling, frieze and cornice are delineated in closely related shades of paint.

Different types of white tend to suit different styles of interior. Among the darker shades of white,

RIGHT *Ben Pentreath's London flat, just round the corner from his office, also features 18th-century panelling, here in his living room painted 'Wimborne White' and a background to his collection of 20th-century art.*

BELOW *The room also retains its original marble fireplace, but has been divided by a wall just behind the sofa to make a separate kitchen. The cream rug is a textured version of the 'Wimborne White' walls and flourishes of colour are introduced in accessories such as the cushions and lamp and the bright stripes of book spines.*

those that work best in more modern, hard-edged interiors are the slightly colder whites such as 'Blackened' and 'Strong White'. Softer and warmer whites with a hint of yellow, which include 'White Tie', 'New White' and 'Matchstick', suit more rustic interiors, while neutral whites with a cooler feel like 'Old White', 'Off-White' and 'Slipper Satin' have a sophisticated air that complements elegant, formal spaces.

White paint has the power to transform, as anyone facing a grubby kitchen or a dingy bathroom with a small budget and a pot of paint can confirm. And the magic of white need not be confined to the architectural shell. Interior designer Nicky Haslam insists that almost any piece of furniture, from a dining-room chair to a bedroom wardrobe, can be transformed into something chic and desirable with a coat of white paint. George Carter puts fresh botanical prints in wooden frames coated with a thin layer of 'Off-White', rubbed back with wire wool and sealed with wax polish. A flat moulding painted with white emulsion makes a sharp, modern surround for a black and white photograph or a contemporary print.

Although this is a chapter about interiors in shades of white, it should also be noted that certain whites are better matches for darker colours than others, according to the predominance of the various pigments that have been added to them. A ceiling painted

ABOVE *Photographer Joanna Vestey's house near the sea in Cornwall has light pouring in from every side and from above. Rooms flow one into the other from generous landings so that it feels almost open plan when doors are not shut. The whole house is painted in shades of white; here on the landing above the kitchen the walls are 'Joa's White' and the skirting boards are 'Slipper Satin'.*

RIGHT *Dermot and Tessa Coleman's kitchen, dining and living room combined occupies the space that was once a grand double drawing room. The sofas are upholstered in ticking and a patchwork of antique linen. Red and blue velvet cushions glow against the 'Strong White' paintwork.*

THIS PAGE *The owners of this 18th-century terraced house in South London have decorated and furnished its beautifully proportioned rooms in contemporary style with minimal clutter. The raised ground floor, originally a formal reception room, is now a sleek kitchen and dining room with a new oak floor. Raised cupboards on either side of the chimney breast hide all the things that would otherwise spoil the effect. Walls and woodwork are painted 'All White', a clean, modern white but without the chemical brighteners that give brilliant whites their cold, blue tinge.*

in ordinary brilliant white will not enhance many of the colours in the Farrow & Ball palette, tending to make them look murky in comparison and detracting from their quality. This may not be immediately obvious to the unpractised eye and finding exactly the right white to go with your chosen colour can be challenging. Fortunately, there are Farrow & Ball colour consultants who can advise on the best pairings, ensuring that whatever your favourite colour, it will be shown off to perfection by the white that suits it best.

RIGHT *The top floor of the same house comprises two spare bedrooms, a bathroom and an office. This sunny space, with its views of trees and houses below, has been painted 'All White' all over, including the original floorboards, the stair banisters and the ceilings. The single paint colour unifies the separate rooms and increases the sense of space, creating a seamless background for sparse but carefully chosen furnishings, such as this natural oak table that holds a spiral of pebbles.*

WALLPAPER AND PAINT SCHEMES

FAR LEFT *Wallpapers in shades of off-white introduce subtle pattern and texture into an all-white room. 'Rosslyn' is adapted from a 19th-century English cotton print and has the delicacy of lace in this pale colourway. Woodwork in 'Pointing', with fractionally darker 'Clunch' as an accent, creates a warm, pretty scheme.*

1 Walls, Rosslyn BP 1906
2 Woodwork, Pointing
3 Accent, Clunch

LEFT *A more traditional floral design, 'St Antoine', taken from an 18th-century French damask, has a modern edge in this subtle colour combination. 'Lime White' and 'Old White' are both warm grey tones that contribute to the sophisticated feel of this scheme.*

1 Walls, St Antoine BP 903
2 Woodwork, Lime White
3 Accent, Old White

ABOVE *Ben Pentreath chose the soft grey of 'Hardwick White' as an elegantly architectural background for his collection of plaster casts. The colour below the dado is 'Shaded White'.*

ABOVE LEFT *A matt neutral such as 'Mouse's Back', the perfect shade of taupe, throws the glossy brilliance of scarlet lacquer and bottle-green silk damask into gorgeous relief.*

LEFT *Shades of grey articulate the architecture in this flat. The hall is 'Hardwick White', a colour that goes round the corner and across the chimney breast, where it modulates to darker 'Chemise'.*

RIGHT *A pale lemon yellow vase on a marble mantelshelf dances with light against a backdrop of shadowy 'Chemise'.*

IN NEUTRAL

'Neutral' can sound dull, neither one thing nor the other, a bit of a cop-out, an

engine idling waiting to get into gear and go somewhere exciting. Nonetheless, neutral is

the accepted term to describe a palette that has been at the top of the colour charts for at least

a decade. These are earthy, natural, gentle colours, the browns of wood, leather and sand, the

greys of stone and sky, overlapping with the darker off-whites, like tawny 'String' and dusky

'Shaded White'. Easy to live with, elegant, undemanding, they merit a more evocative word.

ABOVE *Architect Chris Dyson lives in an early 18th-century house in East London that he saved from dereliction and restored to elegant, classical simplicity. Colours throughout the house are the shades of 'drab' that were fashionable when the house was built. Here, walls are 'London Stone'.*

ABOVE RIGHT *In the same house, 'London Stone' is used on the walls above the panelling going up the staircase, one of the few original features of the building that has survived almost intact. The panelling is painted 'Mouse's Back' and the floor, also in authentic period style, consists of bare, scrubbed boards.*

LEFT *The living room mixes period features with antique, vintage and modern furnishings. Walls, from skirting boards to cornice including the window embrasure and shutters, are 'French Gray', an elusive tone that looks green in some lights, grey in others.*

Contemporary designers may like to think they have invented this way of decorating with its emphasis on natural materials and the colours inspired by them, but before the 18th century, it was traditional for paint colours to be as close as possible to the materials they were covering and protecting. Shades of 'drab' representing stone and wood characterized the paintwork of 16th- and 17th-century interiors, contrasting with the white paint that coated white plaster. In the case of great houses, these colours were a background as opposed to a colour scheme, a humble foil for the vibrancy of wall hangings; tapestries, painted cloth or gilded and embossed leather panels. In poorer homes, however, with their paucity of possessions, the effect might have been almost modern in its sepia severity.

Certainly, much of the appeal of the neutral palette is its affinity with the plain and unadorned, whether unbleached linen or polished wood. The recent fashion for these colours has accompanied a renewed interest in handcrafted furnishings and a preference for the organic over the artificial. Leather has

returned as a popular upholstery material, polished hardwoods have taken the place of painted finishes in couture kitchens and limestone flooring has spread its expensive creamy sheen through halls, kitchens and bathrooms.

Natural materials that have been enhanced by polish and craftsmanship rather than denatured by over-processing have an enduring attraction. Wood and leather, linen and stone link us to a past when the chairs we sat on were made from trees that we may have sheltered under, our blankets woven in wool sheared from sheep in surrounding fields. In lives dominated by screens, our hands in continual contact with plastic, our eyes bathed in synthetic light, it is little wonder that we like to feel cool stone under our feet or enjoy the faint animal smell of tanned leather, the fresh hay tang of seagrass.

So far, so simple and wholesome. In fact, far from being a fail-safe route to an effortlessly stylish interior, a neutral colour scheme is surprisingly easy to get wrong. Consider the colour beige and all that it conjures: seventies safari suits; the leather seats of swanky sports cars; the plastic carcasses of old computers; textured wallpaper the consistency of porridge. The same applies to grey, the wrong shades of which can be as cold and institutional as a prison corridor. When it comes to man-made colour, it seems it is almost easier to come up with a nasty neutral than a nice one. At their synthetic worst these are harsh, dreary, depressing colours to live with. But at their best they are subtle, complex, hard to pin down and as soothing as a mother's hand.

ABOVE LEFT *Panelled walls in one of the second floor bedrooms are in 'Elephant's Breath', another gentle, elusive shade of grey, mixed and brilliantly christened by decorator John Fowler. The door is in 'Mahogany', again appropriate to the period of the house when the fashion was to paint materials, whether wood or stone, in a colour that approximated to their natural state. Touches of modernity — the over-door shelving and the brushed stainless steel door handle — slot seamlessly into the period setting.*

LEFT *All shades of white are relative. In this cottage bathroom belonging to garden designer Jan Howard, 'Hardwick White', which can look surprisingly bright when used over large areas and contrasted with dark, strong colours, shows its distinctly grey tones in comparison with the pure, shiny white of the washbasin. Woodwork is in 'Pointing', here looking decidedly creamy, again in comparison with the sanitary ware.*

THIS PAGE *The main bedroom in Chris Dyson's house is on the first floor behind the sitting room. Here, the panelling is in the shape of cupboards that form an alcove for the four-poster bed and provide essential storage space. The wall colour is again 'French Gray', providing visual continuity between this room and the living room with which it interconnects through the door on the left. The bright red lamp is an automatic focal point because red is a colour that appears to advance towards the eye.*

LEFT *Upholsterer Aiveen Daly's house is characterized by pale and neutral wall colours against which plush fabrics in glorious technicolour create splashes of brilliance. In her bedroom the headboard upholstered in smoky blue velvet to her own design stands against walls in 'Lamp Room Gray'. The cushion and lampshades provide bright spots of buttercup yellow, while the stool picks up the shade and adds a burst of other colours. Grey is a highly effective foil for stronger colours, throwing them into relief, just as shadow contrasts with sunlight.*

When colours are 'natural' and quiet, as opposed to visually arresting, the eye concentrates harder on the qualities of materials and becomes more acutely aware of texture. Imitation stone, vinyl masquerading as leather or plastic as wood can all undermine the effect of a neutral colour scheme as surely as an ill-judged palette. Conversely, the real thing, such as a marble fireplace, an oak floor or a sofa upholstered in pure wool, will look its best and enhance the sense of restrained luxury that neutral colours create.

This is why it is particularly important when decorating with neutrals to use the best-quality paints. Farrow & Ball's selection of neutral shades is second to none. In addition to the comprehensive range of browns and greys at the core of the neutral palette, all the other colour groups, from red, to green, to blue, to yellow, include colours that would also qualify as neutral, whether the soft terracotta of 'Dutch Pink', the light honey of 'Farrow's Cream' or the pale sage of 'Ball Green'. Pigments include titanium dioxide (white) and iron oxides, which are a key component of ochres, umbers and siennas. These pigments have been used by artists for centuries, ground to a powder and mixed with oils or egg white. Farrow & Ball paints also contain chalk, china clay and other minerals. These help to give the different finishes an organic, almost handmade quality that applies to the surface feel of the paint and wallpaper as much as to its depth of colour.

FAR LEFT *Conrad Roeber and David Townsend chose 'Chemise' as the ideal shade of grey against which to display their collection of monochrome prints, drawings and paintings. A long shelf across the back wall of their living room also provides space to display unusual objects such as this articulated hand and pair of wooden shoe trees.*

LEFT *In the dining room of Sophie Conran's 18th-century country house the panelled walls are painted in 'Strong White' and the window embrasures, window seats and shutters in 'Elephant's Breath'. Sophie has added cushions upholstered in a golden yellow woven fabric by Kathryn Ireland. Grey and yellow, like sunlight and shade, have an affinity that means they flatter each other, the grey bringing a refined sophistication to the mix, the yellow preventing the grey from seeming sombre or severe.*

THIS PAGE *Contemporary furnishings become more visually intriguing thanks to their period setting in Alison Hill and John Taylor's first floor drawing room. Grounded by original floorboards stained dark with a glossy finish, the room's palette of neutral colours with highlights of mustard yellow and sharp, acid green is as modern as the L-shaped sofa. So too is the use of 'Chemise' to make a feature of the fireplace wall in a room where all other paintwork is 'All White'.*

Many Farrow & Ball neutrals are based on historic precedent. 'Lamp Room Gray' is taken from the grey distemper used on the walls of the room where oil lamps were stored in Calke Abbey, Derbyshire – one of the best preserved grand Victorian interiors in England. 'Mouse's Back' and 'Dauphin' are based on early 18th-century shades of 'drab', original examples of which survive in attic rooms and servants' quarters. 'Elephant's Breath' is a match for the warm, misty grey invented and named by John Fowler, while the notorious 'Dead Salmon' is a quote from an 1805 painting bill at Kedleston Hall; the 'dead' refers to the paint's matt finish, the salmon to its pinkish tinge.

A decorative scheme using only neutrals can be sophisticated or insipid and its success will depend on how well the different shades harmonize. Neutrals are at their best used with others of similar tones. Some have a touch of yellow and these tend to create a more rustic, informal look. 'String', 'Fawn' and 'Cat's Paw' fit this category and work well with woodwork in 'White Tie', a creamy white. Neutrals with a tinge of lilac, such as 'Skimming Stone' and

LEFT *Ben Pentreath's architectural practice Working Group is based in Bloomsbury, its offices occupying a Georgian house complete with original plasterwork cornices and fireplaces. The ceiling is 'All White', while walls are the pale stone of 'Clunch', a traditional colour scheme for a classical interior of this date.*

BELOW LEFT *The entrance to the offices is a narrow flagged passage that links the front door to the original staircase. The panelled wall to the left and the walls opposite are 'Stony Ground'.*

RIGHT *The classical theme continues in Ben's country retreat, the wing of a contemporary 18th-century style house in Dorset. The drawing room is painted in 'Bone', a cool, elegant neutral, above the dado and 'Shaded White', a very slightly paler neutral, below. Strong colours, such as the reds and blues of cushions, are potent against the pale, earthy shades.*

BELOW *The strict palette of browns, blacks, greys and creams in the entrance hall with walls in 'Hardwick White', is warmed by the red of kilims underfoot.*

'Elephant's Breath', have a clean, more urban feel. The two other groupings of neutrals are those with a red base, including 'Pointing' and 'Joa's White', colours that are warm yet modern, and those with a warm, grey base, 'Slipper Satin', 'Lime White' and 'Old White', which are traditional and elegant in feel.

Contemporary, neutral schemes tend to use plain colours, relying on variations in texture for visual detail and interest. Fabrics in muted stripes and checks fit well in this sort of scheme, in which overt pattern can ruffle the surface and disturb the calm. Another way to introduce pattern is to use wallpaper. Farrow & Ball wallpaper designs come in a wide range of complementary colours, and although the effect of wallpaper tends to be traditional, even their grandest design, 'Silvergate', which is based on an 18th-century damask, takes on a modern feel in shades of taupe. Neutral colourways have the opposite effect on contemporary designs such as 'Bamboo' and 'Lotus', rendering them gentle enough to look at home in a period setting.

All colours are affected by light – both its quality and intensity – but neutrals are particularly susceptible. Farrow & Ball's International Colour Consultant, Joa Studholme, describes how cool, blue-based neutrals sing in the morning light, while those with a red base create a cozy look at sunset. She also advises avoiding green-based neutrals in a north-facing room: 'Yellow-based colours will always make a room feel more sunny.'

Even the most expertly judged palette of neutral colours benefits from contrast. This can be as understated as a vase of snowdrops or a mustard yellow bookbinding. Strong, rich colours glow against shades

ABOVE *Artist Sandra Whitmore's kitchen is a high-ceilinged lean-to built against the back wall of an ancient timber-framed cottage. The flooring in reclaimed brick links the older part of the building to the more recent extension, as does the wall colour, which is 'Pointing'. Colanders, some of which are seen next to the fridge, are one of the things Sandra collects.*

RIGHT *In the staircase hall of William Palin's Regency house the walls are 'Light Stone' and the skirting boards beneath their mouldings are 'Off-Black', a detail he copied from a Regency painting of an interior showing a similar treatment.*

FAR RIGHT *The kitchen of this house decorated by Lulu Carter has cupboards painted in two tones of neutral, 'London Stone' and paler 'Off-White'. Walls are 'Savage Ground'. The blind, limestone flooring and tiles are also in neutrals, against which the darker work surfaces and Aga make a strong contrast.*

of brown and grey, as if thrown into relief by their own shadows. Red is a particularly effective highlight in a neutral room, advancing towards the eye and creating a natural focal point; just as the painter Constable used red horse blankets or a figure wearing a red jacket to punctuate the soft greens and browns of his famous landscapes. Sharper, acid colours – cool lime greens or petrol blues – create a contemporary effect, slicing through the gentleness of a receding neutral with crisp precision. Neutrals are equally effective at softening

ABOVE *Guest bedrooms on the top floor of a luxurious, newly built country house decorated by Emma Sims-Hilditch are furnished with a pretty combination of ginghams and embroidered sprigs from Chelsea Textiles. Walls in 'Dimity', a warm, creamy off-white, pick up the background colour of the fabrics and contribute to the charming, rustic feel that contrasts with the grandeur of rooms on the floors below.*

LEFT *Karen Harrison disguised the crumbling walls of her bathroom with fake matchboarding made from scored sheets of MDF painted in 'Pigeon', a grey that can look green or blue depending on the light. The finish is dead flat oil.*

RIGHT *This new country house has every modern convenience despite its traditional design, including a larder with ample storage opening off the central kitchen. The fitted dresser is painted in 'Pigeon', the walls are 'Slipper Satin' and the rest of the woodwork is 'Off-White'.*

the stark contrast of black and white, providing a flattering foil to prints and engravings or knocking back the stiff geometry of a black and white tiled floor.

Few colour groups have such potential for extremes of glamour and dowdiness. At one end of the spectrum is the sophisticated neutral interior, a symphony of pleasing, gentle colour; restrained, muted, elegant. At the other is the beige three-piece suite teamed with porridge wallpaper. A punishment at my husband's school was to write 1,000 words on the subject of beige. If you have got this far, you have already read some 1,500 words on the subject and its brown and grey relations. But as we know, not all beiges are equal.

ABOVE *George Carter designed this bureau for his clients' country house in Norfolk, adding a top half of panelled cupboard doors and shelving onto an old desk and marrying the two with paint. The inside of the cupboard is 'Green Smoke', a favourite colour that George often uses for garden furniture. The rest is 'Slipper Satin' dragged over with 'Pavilion Gray' by specialist painter Paola Cumiskey.*

RIGHT *Garden designer Jan Howard has created a sophisticated cottage bathroom with a dark wooden floor, walls in 'Hardwick White' and woodwork in 'Pointing'. The red striped chair and cushion introduce comfort and warmth to a scheme that could otherwise feel too austere.*

LEFT *This palatial first floor drawing room in central London, decorated by Diana Sieff, was once a ballroom. Leaf greens teamed with tones of cream, the glint of gilding and a background paint colour of warm 'Matchstick' create a light, airy atmosphere that feels as fresh as a spring morning.*

THIS PAGE *As in her bathroom on the previous page, Jan Howard has used hot reds and pinks, here a pair of silk cushions, to invigorate a room dominated by neutral shades, including the natural stone of the fireplace, the pale browns of the logs and their wicker basket and the rush seating of the rocking chair. Walls and fitted cupboard are 'Biscuit' and the ceiling is 'New White'.*

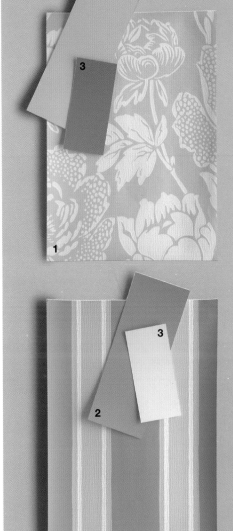

WALLPAPER AND PAINT SCHEMES

ABOVE *A detail of Ben Pentreath's office showing walls in 'Clunch' and ceiling in 'All White'. The flooring is coir matting and the office furniture and computers predominantly black, the only bright colour in the room provided by the rainbow of book spines.*

RIGHT *On the far side of the fireplace in Jan Howard's living room, the contrast between the walls in 'Biscuit' and the ceiling and woodwork in 'New White' is more apparent. Jan's decision to paint the beams the same colour as the plaster, as opposed to the more common and anachronistic black, prevents the room from feeling top-heavy and minimizes the effect of a low ceiling.*

TOP *The woodwork picks up the background colour of this traditional yet contemporary wallpaper, while the darker brown accent contrasts and complements.*

1 Walls, Peony BP 2305
2 Woodwork, Savage Ground
3 Accent, Mouse's Back

BOTTOM *'Block Print Stripe' brings together three colours from the Farrow & Ball range, which can be complemented by woodwork in the same shades.*

1 Walls, Block Print Stripe BP 758
2 Woodwork, Charleston Gray
3 Accent, Skimming Stone

ABOVE RIGHT *Violet and green are always an attractive colour combination. Here, an upholstered headboard and flowery bed linen are placed against walls in 'Ball Green'.*

BELOW *The owner has used 'Oval Room Blue' to differentiate the original wooden panelling in her late Georgian townhouse from the walls and skirting boards in 'Slipper Satin'. The colour is strong enough to make a contrast, but is also soft and receding such that the effect is muted rather than bold.*

FAR RIGHT *The subtle duck-egg of 'Dix Blue' and a skirting board in 'Off-White' make a slightly incongruous setting for an electric guitar in the playroom of a house in Lincolnshire.*

BELOW RIGHT *A cluster of Staffordshire figures and antique mugs and jugs sit on a shelf in Ben Pentreath's country kitchen against walls of 'Ointment Pink', a pale terracotta rather prettier than its name and based on paint scrapings dating back to the beginning of the 19th century.*

THE PALETTE

Ointment Pink®

Setting Plaster®

Calamine®

Pale Powder

Pavilion Blue

Oval Room Blue®

Pigeon®

Blue Gray

Ball Green®

Gervase Yellow®

SOFTLY, SOFTLY

Like the frosted blush of glacé fruits or the pastel sheen of sugared almonds,

faded, gentle colours are the epitome of prettiness. Misty blue, dusty pink, the pale moon

glow of primrose yellow – these are modest, retiring colours that whisper their primary parentage;

happy to hide in the background while other stronger colours seek attention. And shy need not

equal unsophisticated. Forget the usual associations with booties and cradles. Far from twee, at

their subtle best these are some of the most beguiling, versatile colours to decorate a room with.

ABOVE LEFT *Helen Ellery's tiny bedroom is almost filled by an Edwardian oak bedstead, but the colour scheme of walls in 'Pale Powder' with primrose yellow sheets and flowery crewel work curtains is as refreshing as a sea breeze.*

ABOVE RIGHT *Simple wall-hung shelving in one of the bedrooms of Chris Dyson's early Georgian townhouse is painted 'Oval Room Blue', the same colour as the walls and an attractive background for a quirky display of objects, including a vintage tin car and a coloured Regency print. The dark red of the butterfly case looks particularly handsome against this smoky shade of blue.*

Pastel blue and powder pink mark our fate from the moment we are born. So strong are their cultural connotations that it goes against the grain for even the most liberated parents to dress their baby son in a pink bonnet. Sweetly anodyne, these are not colours we would reach for when decorating a drawing room. But, just as there are sour as well as joyful yellows, so there are versions of pale pink and pale blue that are alluring, refined and entirely grown-up.

As is always the case with Farrow & Ball paints, even their palest blues and lightest pinks are shades of depth and distinction saturated with a complex blend of pigments. The difference between a bland pink and an interesting pink is that between white mixed with a little red, which results in the common-or-garden pale pink of synthetic knitting wool and candyfloss, and white mixed with a little red but also a spot of black and a dash of yellow, with results that are far more visually intriguing.

The strength of Farrow & Ball's range of pastel colours is that they are gentle but also intense, faded but not washed out, soft but never insipid. 'Setting Plaster', for example, is almost pink, almost brown; the colour of a fragile shell or a fading rose petal. 'Light Blue' is one of those chameleon Farrow & Ball shades that one moment looks as blue as a pale summer sky, the next as grey as a wintry sea. Like neutrals, these are elusive colours that change throughout the day, seeming to gain and lose different parts of the spectrum from which they are composed.

THIS PAGE *Double doors lead from the main bedroom through to a top-lit bathroom in this spacious London house. Decorator Diana Sieff has spiced up a muted palette of pale natural wood floors and doors and walls in almost-white 'Pavilion Blue' with bursts of yellow on this pair of 18th-century French chairs.*

Perhaps because of their association with all things infantile, pale, pretty colours have fallen out of favour, to the extent that 'pastel shades' have become synonymous with 'ghastly good taste', in the same way that 'magnolia' bespeaks the bland and the boring. The term pastel derives from the paste made by combining dry artist's pigments with chalk and a binder. Compressed to make crayons, pastels were a popular medium throughout the 18th century and particularly fashionable for portraits. If you want to be inspired by the beauty of pastels, look at the work of artists such as Jean-Baptiste-Siméon Chardin and Rosalba Carriera. The typically soft, slightly smudged effect of the medium evokes the peachy skin of society

THIS PAGE The rich colours of sumptuous antique fabrics, used to make cushions and a bedcover, and the polished mahogany and walnut of the bed and side table are foregrounded by the shadowy, receding green of 'Vert de Terre' in this guest bedroom of a large country house.

RIGHT Walls in soft 'Gervase Yellow' are as bright as most paintwork gets in the bathroom of a house remodelled and decorated by George Carter. Picture frames are painted in 'Off-White'.

FAR RIGHT 'Ball Green', seen here on the walls of a bedroom in Jan Howard's cottage, is a very pale olive, an old-fashioned distemper colour from Farrow & Ball's extensive archives.

beauties, dimpled babies and plump-cheeked children to perfection. And the colours are ravishing.

In the 18th century, and equally inspiring, the brothers Robert and James Adam were masters at using a complex palette of pastel shades to articulate the delicate, neoclassical designs of their elegant interiors. Pastel colours were fashionable for plasterwork ceilings and Robert Adam criticized 'the glare of white, so common in every ceiling (sic)', preferring soft shades of terracotta pink, duck-egg blue and faded green.

RIGHT *'Calamine' will need no introduction to anyone who suffered from childhood rashes. Despite itchy associations, it is a delicious pale pink, used here in Helen Ellery's small ground floor guest bedroom. Red and green, which have a natural affinity, add punch to the prettiness.*

LEFT *This comfortable sitting room on the raised ground floor of a Georgian terraced house in South London is painted in two shades of off-white, walls in 'Slipper Satin' and woodwork in 'White Tie', with the low band of original panelling that runs round the whole room picked out in 'Oval Room Blue'. The trio of gentle paint colours makes a restrained background for antiques and works of art.*

ABOVE LEFT *Dermot and Tessa Coleman have changed the orientation of their house such that guests now enter through a hall at the back of the house. Walls are painted 'Green Blue', a colour that despite the reputation of both its components for being 'cool', is welcoming. It is also a colour that works particularly well with shades of brown, here provided by the seagrass mat and the antique bench.*

LEFT *Dermot and Tessa Coleman's kitchen by Craigie Woodworks is set within the elegant architecture of a space that was designed as a formal drawing room. The room is bathed in light thanks to high ceilings matched by tall windows, a quality enhanced by the colour scheme of walls in 'Strong White' and kitchen units in shades of blue, here 'Oval Room Blue' for a glazed storage cupboard.*

RIGHT *This tiny spare bedroom, and its adjacent shower room, completely fill the back yard behind Helen Ellery's Central London cottage. With buildings on either side, the only possible source of light was from above. Storage space has been maximized by building a bed above deep cupboards, while shelves on simple wooden brackets make use of available wall space. The walls in 'Calamine' give this enclosed space a soft glow like the inside of a shell or the middle of a pale pink rose.*

Few of us will ever face the problem of decorating a grand, neoclassical interior, but what Robert Adam recognized is that pale colours are a flattering foil for the darker tones of pictures and furnishings. The polished wood of antique furniture, the dull glint of old picture frames and the rich lustre of silks and velvets are all shown to advantage by a background of pale colour. Darker tones of the same shade as the pastel, a deep forest green against walls in 'Vert de Terre' or a rich raspberry red with 'Calamine' paintwork, can enhance both the paler and the darker colour. Alternatively, you can create more contrast with pairings of complementary colours, such as a mustard yellow against 'Parma Gray' or deep red against 'Pale Powder'.

Using pastel colours with polished mahogany and gilt creates a traditional look, as in the country house designed by Emma Sims-Hilditch for clients whose furnishings and paintings are mainly antique. A more contemporary effect is achieved by

mixing pastel colours with neutrals, as seen on page 171 in rooms designed by Diana Sieff for a client with a grand London flat. Here, where the drawing room colours are soft greens and browns against creams and off-whites, the effect is clean and streamlined, even though much of the furniture is antique, albeit painted as opposed to polished.

Combinations of pastel shades are a feature of some of the paler colourways in the Farrow & Ball range of wallpapers, where pattern is applied in a slightly darker tone onto a background of a paler one, or vice versa. The closer the tones, the more muted the pattern, however big and bold its design. Choosing a wallpaper that features different tones of the same colour can help to pull together a room scheme, although carefully matching it with curtains and upholstery in the lighter shade and cushions and carpet in the darker one will almost certainly look contrived and stilted. Better to use a wallpaper as a springboard for a colour scheme in sympathetic tones than to echo its colours slavishly.

Colour can be intimidating. Paint a room bright red or deep purple and you are heavily committed, as it is difficult to tone down a space dominated by a single, powerful colour. With a pastel background you can add colour gradually with fabrics, flowers and lamps, controlling and varying its intensity. Cautious yes, but with undeniably pretty results.

LEFT *'Blue Gray' is one of artist Sandra Whitmore's favourite colours for decorating. She has used it on both the inside and outside of her cottage, as she finds it a very peaceful colour.*

BELOW LEFT *This Soho room has the feel of a snug ship's cabin with its sloping walls and matchboarding. Walls are painted 'Pigeon' and the eye-catching red of the pot and the machine mould is picked up in the curtain fabric.*

RIGHT *On either side of the chimney breast in architect William Smalley's London flat are deep storage cupboards where he tucks away the computer, files, books, magazines and papers that would otherwise clutter his serenely empty panelled rooms. The interior of the cupboard on the left is painted in 'Light Blue' and this one is in pale pink 'Setting Plaster'. The combination of colour and content is a pleasing counterpoint to the 'All White' discipline of the rest of the room.*

WALLPAPER AND PAINT SCHEMES

FAR LEFT *Abstract 'Vermicelli' looks modern, but in fact dates back to the 18th century. Here rendered in light-reflecting silver on palest blue, it is teamed with the soft, pale neutrals 'Pavilion Gray' and 'Blackened'. These elegant shades of grey combine particularly elegantly with blue.*

1 Walls, Vermicelli BP 1554
2 Woodwork, Pavilion Gray
3 Accent, Blackened

LEFT *Woodwork in gentle pink 'Setting Plaster' brings out the pink tinge in the background of the 'Ringwold' wallpaper. The warm, pale grey of 'Slipper Satin', used here as an accent, introduces a slightly harder edge.*

1 Walls, Ringwold BP 1618
2 Woodwork, Setting Plaster
3 Accent, Slipper Satin

ABOVE *This tiny entrance hall to a first floor London flat has been transformed by bright red 'Harissa' to make a dramatic introduction to rooms that lead off on either side. No distinction has been made between walls, doors and book shelving, which are all painted the same colour. Framed prints echo the scarlet paint in spidery, graphic highlights.*

ABOVE MIDDLE *Ben Pentreath has painted the inside of an 18th-century mahogany bureau bookcase bright 'Chinese Blue' as a striking background to a variety of objects, many of them white, that are arranged on the shelves.*

ABOVE RIGHT *An antique bowl against walls in 'Octagon Yellow' makes a pleasingly simple still life.*

RIGHT *The combination of dark wood furnishings, dark floorboards and glossy leather upholstery in an elegant ground floor reception room painted 'Octagon Yellow' is handsome and typically Regency, as befits the date of this house.*

FAR RIGHT *'Rectory Red' is the shade of red that art critic John Ruskin thought most suitable for the display of oil paintings, which is one of the reasons art collectors Dermot and Tessa Coleman chose it for their drawing room.*

Rectory Red®

Incarnadine

Blazer®

Orangery

Babouche®

Octagon Yellow®

Churlish Green

Arsenic®

Pea Green

Stone Blue®

BRIGHT & BEAUTIFUL

There is something both brave and joyful about painting a room a bold, bright colour.

Whether a fresh green lawn, a big blue sky or the façade of a building painted orange,

expanses of strong colour evoke an emotional response and this is just as true of an

interior as a landscape. Who can fail to be uplifted by a room that glows with smiling,

sunny yellow, feel cocooned by walls in ruby red or refreshed by an energetic blue?

'A certain blue enters your soul. A certain red has an effect on your blood pressure,' said Henri Matisse. The link between colour and emotion has a long history, if few definitive rules. It is broadly agreed that 'cool', 'receding' colours at the green and blue end of the spectrum are soothing and tranquil, and that 'warm', 'advancing' colours in the range between red and yellow are exciting and stimulating. The brighter a colour, the more likely a response. However, there are so many variations within each colour group beyond the primary school basics of red, yellow and blue – acid yellows and orange yellows, lime greens and olive greens, blue-tinged reds and brown-tinged reds – that it is impossible to make sweeping statements without much of the truth getting lost under the carpet. Hence Matisse's careful use of the word 'certain'.

ABOVE AND ABOVE RIGHT
Ben Pentreath has alternated bright,
bold colour with more neutral schemes
in his London flat – scarlet 'Harissa'
in his entrance hall, opening into a
living room on one side in 'Wimborne
White', with an adjacent kitchen in
dark 'Pantalon' and a bedroom on the
other in 'Shaded White' leading into
this sharp 'Arsenic' green bathroom.
Framed antique maps pick up the
green and also echo the bright red
of the towel.

RIGHT *William Palin has used*
'Stone Blue' for bathrooms in both
his houses. Bathrooms are a modern
imposition in pre-20th-century homes,
making the more contemporary feel
of this intense shade an appropriate
choice. Delft tiles from the 17th
century are propped on the basin
as a makeshift splashback.

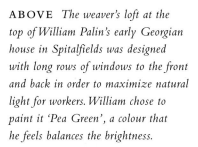

ABOVE *The weaver's loft at the*
top of William Palin's early Georgian
house in Spitalfields was designed
with long rows of windows to the front
and back in order to maximize natural
light for workers. William chose to
paint it 'Pea Green', a colour that
he feels balances the brightness.

Had he been more verbose, Matisse might have added 'a certain blue used in a certain way, in a certain place'. Context is also crucial to the effect of colour. William Palin's beautifully proportioned Regency house featured in the 'Classical' chapter at the beginning of this book (pp16–21) is a fine example of strong and contrasting colours used in adjacent rooms to give what he memorably calls an 'episodic effect'. These are big, high-ceilinged spaces awash with daylight that pours through tall sash windows, unimpeded by curtains. Less intense versions of the reds, yellows, blues and greens that William has chosen would have been bleached out by so much light and space. As it is, 'India Yellow', 'Book Room Red', 'Stone Blue' and 'Pea Green' bring warmth and life to a house that might otherwise feel too spartan for comfort. It is almost as if the colours furnish the room.

Architect Ben Pentreath has been similarly forthright with colour in the very different setting of his flat, on the first floor of an early 18th-century house in Bloomsbury, London. The entrance hall is not much bigger than a telephone box, so it is perhaps appropriate that Ben has painted it floor to ceiling in 'Harissa', an archive colour that is the scarlet of hunting

ABOVE *The owner of this Georgian London house chose rosy 'Incarnadine' for a bedroom in the attic. The cottage proportions of the room, added to the warmth of colour, have a comforting, cocooning effect on those lucky enough to sleep in it.*

LEFT *Another small space punching well above its weight thanks to bold colour, in this instance the entrance hall of Ben Pentreath's London flat. Looking through the hall from the off-white bedroom to the off-white living room, echoes of red make a visual link between the three spaces, whether the bed linen, hallway carpet or the cushions on the sofa.*

FAR LEFT *At the far end of the hall in Jo Berryman's terraced London house she has created a small, eye-catching study space with a desk, chair and shelving decorated in hot red. Shelves are painted in eggshell 'Rectory Red' and the walls are papered in 'Bamboo' in black on the same red background.*

ABOVE *Instead of unifying the two first floor reception rooms that lead one into the other in his London house, William Palin has painted the front drawing room in 'Octagon Yellow' and the back study in 'Book Room Red', separating the colours in a neat stripe down the leading edge of the double doors. Both colours have an almost edible quality; 'Book Room Red' is like strawberries mixed with cream, while 'Octagon Yellow' is the colour of Dijon mustard. Luckily, the visual mix works much better than the flavours would.*

LEFT AND RIGHT *Helen Ellery loves shades of green and has used two in her kitchen: 'Pigeon' for the kitchen units and the brighter, almost-yellow 'Churlish Green' on the wooden panelling on the wall next to the table.*

jackets, holly berries and old-fashioned telephone boxes. In this confined space, illuminated by borrowed light from rooms either side, the colour feels so concentrated it almost hums. Painted white, this space would be ordinary; in vibrant red it is a little piece of theatre.

These examples show how difficult it is to be prescriptive about colour, especially of the more conspicuous variety. Opinions are almost certain to be divided, particularly over stronger colours. On a practical level, a deep, bright colour is harder to paint over if you decide that you have made a mistake. For this reason it is wise to take care when choosing it. A patchwork of sample pot squares painted on one wall will not be evidence enough. Better to paint as large a piece of cardboard as you can find and prop it in different places in the room you are intending to decorate so that you can see how the colour reacts at different times of the day and under artificial light. Some bright colours come into their own after dark, especially when lit by the golden haloes of candle flames. William Palin chose 'Calke Green' for his London dining room with candlelight very much in mind.

For centuries, bright, lasting colour that was affordable and that did not decay and fade was a luxury. Blue paint was rarely used in interiors before the beginning of the 18th century when Prussian blue was developed. Brunswick green, a copper compound, was invented later in the century and chrome yellow in the early 19th century. Today, we are spoilt for choice but also dominated by synthetic colour that can be crude and tiresome. This is never true of a Farrow & Ball colour. 'Cook's Blue', 'Arsenic', 'Babouche', 'Blazer' and many more are as subtly beautiful as they are bright.

ABOVE *The smaller the room, the brighter the colour in this Norfolk house by George Carter. Buttercup yellow 'Babouche' makes a chic contrast with a set of black and white engravings in the downstairs cloakroom.*

WALLPAPER AND PAINT SCHEMES

FAR LEFT *Bright colour married with the large-scale design of 'Lotus' creates an effect as bold as it is sumptuous. 'Churlish Green' woodwork picks up the pattern of the wallpaper, while accents in 'London Clay' ground the scheme with a darker shade of brown.*

1 Walls, Lotus BP 2048
2 Woodwork, Churlish Green
3 Accent, London Clay

LEFT *Romantic and lush, life-size 'Wisteria' would glamorize any room. Used as an accent on one wall, or all over for even greater impact, it is complemented in this colourway by woodwork in 'Cinder Rose', and accents in 'Charleston Gray'.*

1 Walls, Wisteria BP 2209
2 Woodwork, Cinder Rose
3 Accent, Charleston Gray

ABOVE *Dark colours can transform the mundane and ordinary by conjuring theatrical glamour. Here, the effect of 'Studio Green' on walls and woodwork is given an added layer of visual mystery by the use of mirror glass to back alcoves on either side of the fireplace.*

ABOVE RIGHT *Jo Berryman has used earthy 'Dauphin' in her kitchen as a foil to bright red – her fridge and coat, but also the red of her chairs and gingham tablecloth.*

RIGHT *'Pea Green' is a colour that tends to absorb light when used over large areas. It is teamed here with almost-black 'Studio Green' on the window frames in a weaver's loft so thoroughly flooded with daylight that the room feels intimate rather than gloomy.*

FAR RIGHT *Used in large rooms with generous windows and plenty of natural light, a dusky colour like this 'Book Room Red' is confident without being overpowering.*

THE PALETTE

Picture Gallery Red®

Pelt®

Brinjal®

Tanner's Brown®

Hague Blue®

Studio Green®

Green Smoke®

Down Pipe

Off-Black

London Clay

DARK & HANDSOME

It remains a typical act of teenage rebellion to want a bedroom painted black.

Rather than recoiling in horror, despairing parents might consider the fact that Lutyens,

one of our greatest architects, had a black drawing room, set off by apple green floorboards and

red lacquer furniture, while society decorator David Hicks painted his drawing room walls a colour

he christened 'Coca-cola'. Presumably, teenagers feel that dark colours are appropriately moody.

And they are right in thinking that a dark colour can create a sophisticated effect.

LEFT AND BELOW LEFT *The kitchen of Ben Pentreath's London flat is a long, narrow space sliced off the panelled drawing room. As in the tiny entrance hall, which he has painted scarlet, Ben has chosen a bold colour to give the room distinction and character, rather than attempting to fight the lack of space with a light-reflecting shade of white. Dark brown 'Pantalon' looks smart and crisp contrasted with white tiles, crockery and paintwork, and makes a strong backdrop for the framed posters that reflect Ben's love of graphic art and lettering.*

RIGHT *Architect Chris Dyson has picked out the door and architrave on the first floor of his early Georgian house in 'Mahogany', a period colour popular in the 17th and early 18th century for its approximation to the colour of dark wood. The walls are 'French Gray' and the staircase walls are 'London Stone'.*

Dark colours are the modal jazz of the decorator's palette; redolent of husky voices, smoky bars, trysts and secrets, lipstick and whisky. Walls painted or papered in deep, rich shades create an indoor twilight as atmospheric and evocative as a stage set. On a bright summer's day, the room will vibrate with absorbed sunlight, while in the low light of table lamps or the yellow flicker of candlelight, the same space becomes a glimmering chiaroscuro of shadowy corners and pools of glowing colour.

At the opposite end of the Farrow & Ball colour chart from 'All White' are three shades of black. Blackest of all is 'Pitch Black'. Its neighbours are 'Off-Black' and 'Black Blue'. All three are virtually indistinguishable from one another until used over a large area when it becomes apparent that 'Off-Black' is a softer black, and 'Black Blue' is definitely blue. Almost as dark are 'Studio Green', 'Railings' and 'Hague Blue', all of which look black until painted on a wall, when their respective green, bronze and blue tints become apparent. 'Pelt' similarly hints at red; 'Tanner's Brown' is the colour of peat.

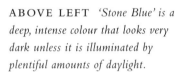

ABOVE LEFT *'Stone Blue' is a deep, intense colour that looks very dark unless it is illuminated by plentiful amounts of daylight.*

ABOVE RIGHT *William Palin chose 'Calke Green' for the ground floor dining room of his London house because it looks so handsome in candlelight. This is probably because greens and blues are the last colours our eyes are able to distinguish in low light conditions.*

LEFT *Garden designer Jan Howard restored her cottage on the Cowdray Estate while also working on the restoration of the walled Tudor garden and derelict stable block, and found the carved fire surround that is now the centrepiece of her study in an outbuilding. This room, which is also a library, is the ultimate evening retreat, with the open fire casting a glow on the sombre 'Studio Green' walls and candlelight reflected by the mirrored alcoves.*

Choosing to use one of these powerful shades on every wall of a room is choosing to sacrifice reflected light and illusions of space in favour of sombre glamour and warm enclosure. This works best in rooms that are already starved of natural light, where instead of fighting the existing gloom with an optimistic all-over white you can instead embrace it and make a virtue of its drama. Add mirrors and an open fire, as in Jan Howard's 'Studio Green' sitting room, and you have a night-time retreat both cozy and mysterious, glass darkly glittering, walls fading into the unknown and unseen.

Contrast is always visually exciting and using dark colours to differentiate between spaces is a certain way to create interior theatre. Most striking of all is the sensation of emerging from a dark, confined space into volume and light. This is the effect created by James Soane and Christopher Ash in their urban flat where they have painted their windowless entrance hall, including doors and the ceiling, in 'Railings', such that walking through it from their front door into the long, bright main room feels like walking from night into day. Dermot and Tessa Coleman have conjured similar magic by painting a north-facing, dark wood-panelled gallery that links their staircase hall with their kitchen in 'Bible Black', a velvety deep purple. The soaring ceiling, tall windows and off-white paintwork of the kitchen beyond are uplifting after this richly shadowy interlude.

ABOVE *Jan Howard is fortunate to have a whole room, albeit a tiny one, in which to store magazines. By installing an L-shaped fitted bench well upholstered with cushions next to the shelving, she has made this enclosed space somewhere you might also wish to read them. Walls are warm 'Wainscot'; windows are 'Biscuit'.*

ABOVE RIGHT *'Book Room Red' has quite a different feel in the attic bedroom of William Palin's Regency house from its effect in the more grandly proportioned study. Here it is comfortable as opposed to imposing.*

RIGHT *This well-appointed new country house has a brick-floored wine cellar and apple store painted 'Picture Gallery Red' – handsome enough for entertaining. The 'Mahogany'-painted side table is by Neptune Classics.*

Deep colour is a fabulous background for pictures that is flattering to oil paintings and prints alike. It also flatters furnishings, whether polished antiques that glint tantalizingly in the general gloom or pieces chosen deliberately to stand out from the darkness – perhaps an oriental bowl in zingy celadon green or the contemporary silhouette of a white Verner Panton chair. A single wall painted a dark colour can provide enough in the way of sharp contrast to animate a room. This could be a fireplace wall throwing the white marble of a chimney piece into sharp relief or the wall behind a bed wallpapered to create a dark frame for a carved or upholstered bedhead. James Soane and Christopher Ash have used 'Railings' on one wall of their main living room in a continuation of the entrance hall. Pictures, furniture and ornaments seem to glow against the grey, drawing and entertaining the eye. The glamour of dark colours translates particularly well to wallpaper, which, like paint, can be used either to envelop a room in dusky pattern or on a single wall as an eye-catching feature.

A less ostentatious trick is to use dark colours to pick out architectural details. Karen Harrison has outlined skirting boards, architraves, shutters and the woodwork of an internal window in 'Down Pipe', an inversion of the more usual darker walls with lighter woodwork that she copied from houses seen on her travels. The result is crisp and an effective way to highlight the good proportions and detailing of her 18th-century interior. William Palin deploys 'Off-Black' in a similar way along the base of the skirting boards in his house, an idea he translated from a painting of a Regency interior. The colour both grounds and articulates

the woodwork, and gives a pleasing juncture between walls and floors. He has also used 'Off-Black' in more practical ways, as a painted line in place of a skirting board in the rear hall and as painted fingerplates on the kitchen cupboards to disguise grubby fingermarks.

Ways not to use dark paint are on the ceiling in a room painted in lighter colours or on the walls above an expanse of dado in a lighter colour. Using dark layered above light creates an uncomfortable sensation of heaviness, like a building resting on flimsy stilts. Using dark colours lower in a room, on the floor, skirtings or below the dado, has the opposite effect, making a space feel safe and anchored.

Dark colours are particularly susceptible to the effects of different finishes. Matt black paint seems to eat light, while the high gloss of a shiny black front door reflects as much light as it absorbs. The silky sheen of eggshell lies between the two. This is the finish of Farrow & Ball's floor paint and is a clever way to use a dark colour with the surprising effect of making the floor look wider and the space above it lighter and more voluminous.

TOP *Emma Sims-Hilditch has used 'Studio Green' on the metal banisters of this staircase in a new country house as a subtle alternative to black.*

ABOVE *Downstairs lavatories are traditionally the place to be experimental and quirky with decoration. William Palin has used his to diversify from more traditional colours to the dramatic deep purple of 'Brinjal', which despite appearances dates back to the 19th century.*

WALLPAPER AND PAINT SCHEMES

LEFT *Conrad Roeber and David Townsend have created an intriguing and atmospheric room in their top floor Soho flat from an unpromising space with a low ceiling and a single, small window. By panelling the walls with MDF and painting them in 'Railings', a very deep grey with a tinge of bronze, they have given the space the feel of a private, insulated retreat. This table next to the window makes the most of limited natural light.*

ABOVE *A long, partially panelled room with a heavily beamed ceiling and Tudor windows links the inner staircase hall with the kitchen in Dermot and Tessa Coleman's country house. The room faces north and is naturally dark, a characteristic they have turned to theatrical effect by painting the walls above the panelling rich, regal 'Bible Black'. Walls are hung with antique maps and the carpet was commissioned from The Rug Company.*

TOP *Here, the dark, velvety brown of woodwork in 'London Clay' and accents in darker 'Pelt' contrast with the glint of 'Bamboo' in a metallic colourway.*

1 Walls, Bamboo BP 2115
2 Woodwork, London Clay
3 Accent, Pelt

BOTTOM *A dramatic scheme teams a swirling damask with woodwork in nearly-black 'Railings'. 'Parma Gray' looks almost white in comparison.*

1 Walls, Silvergate BP 850
2 Woodwork, Railings
3 Accent, Parma Gray

PAINTS, PAPERS AND MORE

The following glossary aims to answer some of the most frequently asked questions about Farrow & Ball paints and wallpapers, and how to use them.

PAINT FINISHES

INTERIOR FINISHES

Estate® Emulsion

This is the most popular paint for walls and ceilings and has the chalky, matt finish and depth of colour so characteristic of Farrow & Ball paints. Despite appearances, it is wipeable.

Modern Emulsion

Also designed for walls and ceilings, this version of emulsion is completely washable and stain resistant, suitable for kitchens and bathrooms and robust enough for areas of high usage such as halls. It has a slightly higher sheen than Estate® Emulsion.

Estate® Eggshell

Extremely durable and with a low sheen, this is the paint recommended for interior woodwork and metal, including radiators, and is completely washable.

Full Gloss

A traditional high-gloss finish, versatile and robust enough for both interior and exterior wood and metalwork. It can also be used to dramatic effect on interior walls and ceilings.

Floor Paint

With the same low sheen as eggshell, this is a very hard-wearing paint that can be used on wooden or concrete floors. It is not suitable for outdoor use.

Dead Flat

This finish is often chosen by purists for the interior of period houses because of its very traditional matt surface that replicates the look of historic lead-based paints. It is wipeable, but not suitable for use in kitchens and bathrooms.

Dead Flat Varnish

Suitable for interior bare wood and painted wood or metal surfaces, this protective varnish has a classic, matt appearance and is wipeable.

Eggshell Varnish

This can be used in exactly the same way as the Dead Flat Varnish, but has a low sheen and is washable.

The following specialist finishes, suitable for the sympathetic decorating of historic and period interiors, are made to order:

Soft Distemper

Made to a traditional recipe using natural resins, this paint has an exceptionally matt and slightly powdery finish and is breathable. It is suitable for walls and ceilings and is only available in the Farrow & Ball range of off-whites.

Casein Distemper

The addition of casein makes this distemper wipeable and more durable than Soft Distemper. It is also suitable for walls and ceilings, is breathable and available in the full range of colours.

Limewash

One of the oldest types of paint, limewash can be used on walls and ceilings both internally and externally. It is available in a selection of Farrow & Ball colours as indicated on the colour cards.

EXTERIOR FINISHES

Exterior Masonry

A very durable matt paint suitable for outside walls, brickwork and render, and available in over 100 colours. It is also completely washable.

Exterior Eggshell

Designed for exterior use on softwood and hardwood window frames, cladding, garden furniture, railings, gates, guttering and garden furniture, with a high resistance to flaking and peeling.

PRIMERS AND UNDERCOATS

Farrow & Ball make a full range of primers and undercoats, including a Stabilising Primer for porous plaster surfaces, a rust-inhibiting Metal Primer and a Stain Block Primer to block resinous stains on bare hardwoods and softwoods. Interior and Exterior Undercoats come in a range of colours designed to enhance the depth of colour of the topcoat. The appropriate undercoat for each of Farrow & Ball's 132 colours can be found on the colour card or on the website.

COLOUR GROUPS

Some colours work better together than others. Farrow & Ball colour consultants are trained to advise and have far more knowledge and experience than there is space on these pages to include. Most colour schemes, however, use at least one neutral or off-white, whether for the ceiling, the woodwork or as part of an all-white or neutral scheme. It is useful, therefore, to know how Farrow & Ball's exceptional range of these colours divides into four main groups, as listed below.

Warm Grey Tones include 'Slipper Satin', 'Lime White', 'Off-White', 'Old White'.

Yellow Tones include 'White Tie', 'New White', 'Matchstick', 'String'.

Warm Reds include 'Pointing', 'Dimity', 'Joa's White', 'Archive'.

Cool Greys include 'Wimborne White', 'Strong White', 'Skimming Stone', 'Elephant's Breath'.

Farrow & Ball colour consultants can also advise on which shade of neutral or off-white will best flatter any other colour in the range. A brilliant white ceiling can spoil the effect of a wall colour, making it look dingy as opposed to subtle. The way colours interrelate between the different rooms of a house should also be considered, and how they will affect the view from one space into another. Painting all the woodwork the same colour is one way of unifying an interior in which the walls of

separate rooms are painted in different colours. Getting the right balance of colour between rooms is also important. If, from the vantage point of a hall or landing, you can see into rooms with colours of differing intensity – perhaps a soft colour used in one room, and a vibrant, weighty colour in another – the effect will be visually disjointed. Painting a house the same colour throughout may not be very adventurous, but it will amplify the space, in the same way that a single colour of flooring helps space to flow between rooms.

HOW TO USE PAINT TO CHANGE THE PROPORTIONS OF A ROOM

Paint is a powerful tool. It can make a space feel wider, smaller, taller and squarer, and can be used to enhance good proportions and to help disguise bad ones. These effects rely on two visual qualities – contrast, and the difference between receding and advancing colours.

Contrast, or a lack of it, can highlight good architectural features or gloss over less desirable ones. Contrast tends to stop the eye and draw attention to itself. The stronger the contrast between walls and woodwork, the more conscious you become of whatever is delineated by the different colours. If, however, you paint walls and woodwork in the same shade, you can disguise unwanted architectural details and make a space feel bigger. Finishing a wall colour below ceiling height at picture rail level makes the ceiling feel lower, just as continuing a colour up to the ceiling and not making a strong contrast between wall and ceiling lifts the perceived height of a room.

Receding and advancing colours can be useful for changing the proportions of awkward spaces such as long, narrow rooms. Blues and greens are generally receding; reds and yellows advancing. If the wall at one end of a long, narrow room is painted an advancing colour, it will appear to come towards the eye and therefore makes the room seem more square. You can also trick the eye into seeing depth and definition by employing different shades of the same colour, for example by painting the receding fields of a panelled door in a slightly darker shade than the frames that surround them.

Generally speaking, it is better to use darker shades lower down in a room. Painting skirting boards, or a whole floor, in a dark colour will make everything above it seem lighter and more spacious in contrast, whereas a dark ceiling in a light room can feel as if it is falling on your head.

COLOUR AND LIGHT

Colour and light are one and the same thing. As light fades, colour disappears, blue and green being the last colours we are able to distinguish in low levels of light. This is why it is important to consider the intensity and quality of light in a room before deciding what colour to paint it. Northern light makes colours look greener, which is why it is best to avoid cool colours in north-facing rooms. Southern, sunny light adds yellow, bringing its own warmth to any colour scheme.

It is all very well to know this in theory, but to see for yourself, one of the best ways is to paint a large piece of card in any colour you are considering using and watch how it changes throughout the day and when placed in different areas of a room. It is also important to see how it reacts to artificial light and even to candlelight, if it is a dining room for example.

Although light colours will help enhance natural light, sometimes it can be more effective to embrace the enclosed, intimate feel of a room that enjoys little daylight by painting it a dark colour such as a deep red or sultry green. Instead of a room that is a bit less dark, you will create drama and beauty.

Colour can affect the atmosphere of any room. Variations are endless, and also highly personal, but as a broad guideline it is worth remembering that colours with blue and grey tones tend to have a formal feel, while warmer tones of red and yellow can be more cozy and relaxing.

ARCHIVE COLOURS

At any one time there are always 132 colours in the Farrow & Ball range. Over the years some colours have been superseded by newer ones. The colours no longer included in the current chart are known as Archive Colours and are available to order. Featured in this book is a mix of current and Archive colours.

WALLPAPERS

Farrow & Ball wallpapers are made using Farrow & Ball paints and display the same depth and sophistication of colour. All papers have a background colour applied with a brush, giving them a unique textural quality. Pattern is applied by old-fashioned block printing, adding an extra layer of paint on top of the painted background and contributing to the handcrafted feel of the papers. Stripes and drags are trough-printed, another traditional method of production.

The wallpaper collection is extensive and includes a range of stripes and drags. Some patterns, such as 'Lotus' and 'Bamboo', are available in two different scales, and can look strikingly contemporary, especially on a larger scale. There is a wide choice of styles across the collections from traditional damasks – 'Silvergate', 'St Antoine' and 'St Germain' – to florals – 'Uppark', 'Wisteria' and 'Melrose' – and trellis and sprig designs. There are more than 800 colourways, including glimmering metallics, and the full collection can be viewed on the website and in Farrow & Ball showrooms.

All wallpapers are made to order in the same Dorset workshops as the paints. There is a minimum order of three rolls and you can request up to five free A4 samples.

HOW TO ORDER

Most paint is ready to take away from Farrow & Ball showrooms and stockists throughout the world. For an up-to-date list of retailers visit www.farrow-ball.com.

If you need any advice on colours, paint finishes or wallpaper, either visit your nearest Farrow & Ball showroom or stockist, or contact Farrow & Ball on +44 (0)1202 876141; USA 888 511 1121 or Canada 877 363 1040.

PICTURE CREDITS

KEY: **a**=above, **b**=below, **r**=right, **l**=left, **c**=centre.

All photography by Jan Baldwin

Endpapers: 'Wisteria' BP 2213 from The Chelsea Papers collection; **page 1** Jo Berryman's home in London; **2** painting by Taylors Interiors Ltd; **3** the Kent home of William Palin of SAVE Britain's Heritage; **4** Chris Dyson Architects; **5** Ben Pentreath's London office; **6** Ben Pentreath's house in Dorset; **7** Jo Berryman's home in London; **8a** the Kent home of William Palin of SAVE Britain's Heritage; **8b** stylist Karen Harrison's house in East Sussex is available for photo shoots, please contact Emma Davies on 07734 617639; **9** a house in Lincolnshire designed by Lulu Carter Design; **10** the Coleman's family home; **11** a house in the West Country designed by its owners and Emma Sims-Hilditch www.theinterior.co.uk, furniture by Neptune Classics; **12–13** Alison Hill & John Taylor's home in Greenwich, unit by Domus; **14** the London home of William Palin of SAVE Britain's Heritage; **15l** a house in Norfolk designed by George Carter, paint effects by Paola Cumiskey; **15c** & **15r** the Kent home of William Palin of SAVE Britain's Heritage; **16–21** the London home of William Palin of SAVE Britain's Heritage (Blur poster designed by Stylorouge); **22–27** a house in Norfolk designed by George Carter, paint effects by Paola Cumiskey; **28–33** carpentry & joinery by Martin Brown, painting by Taylors Interiors Ltd; **34–39** the Kent home of William Palin of SAVE Britain's Heritage, decorating by Justin Webb & Howard Fisher; **40** the London home of James Soane & Christopher Ash of Project Orange; **41l** Jo Berryman's home in London; **41c, 41r** & **42–45** the London home of Conrad Roeber and David Townsend who run interior design practice Schubart Masters; **46–51** Jo Berryman's home in London; **52–57** the London home of James Soane & Christopher Ash of Project Orange; **58** stylist Karen Harrison's house in East Sussex is available for photo shoots, please contact Emma Davies on 07734 617639; **59l** the Coleman's family home; **59c** & **59r** photographer Joanna Vestey and her husband Steve Brooks' home in Cornwall; **60–65** stylist Karen Harrison's house in East Sussex is available for photo shoots, please contact Emma Davies on 07734 617639; **66–71** sophieconran.com, flowers and arrangements by The Blacksmiths Daughter; **72–77** photographer Joanna Vestey and her husband Steve Brooks' home in Cornwall, kitchen by Plain English; **78** Ben Pentreath's house in Dorset; **79l** & **79c** a house in Lincolnshire designed by Lulu Carter Design; **79r** the Coleman's family home; **80–85** Ben Pentreath's house in Dorset; **86–91** the Coleman's family home; **92–97** a house in the West Country designed by its owners and Emma Sims-Hilditch www.theinterior.co.uk; **98–103** a house in Lincolnshire designed by Lulu Carter Design; **104, 105l** & **105r** artist Sandra Whitmore's cottage; **105c** designer Helen Ellery's home in London; **106–111** artist Sandra Whitmore's cottage, kitchen by Plain English; **112–117** designer Helen Ellery's home in London; **118–119** the London home of William Palin of SAVE Britain's Heritage; **120l** photographer Joanna Vestey and her husband Steve Brooks' home in Cornwall; **120ar** designed by Diana Sieff/Sieff Interiors; **120br** & **121** stylist Karen Harrison's house in East Sussex is available for photo shoots, please contact Emma Davies on 07734 617639; **122–123** Alison Hill & John Taylor's home in Greenwich; **124–125** architect William Smalley's London flat; **126l** Alison Hill & John Taylor's home in Greenwich; **126–127** designed by Diana Sieff/Sieff Interiors; **128–129** the London home of furniture designer and upholsterer Aiveen Daly; **130** Ben Pentreath's London office; **131** both Ben Pentreath's London flat; **132** photographer Joanna Vestey and her husband Steve Brooks' home in Cornwall; **133** the Coleman's family home; **134** & **135a** Alison Hill & John Taylor's home in Greenwich, cupboards by Domus; **136al** designed by Diana Sieff/Sieff Interiors; **136bl** the London home of Conrad Roeber and David Townsend who run

interior design practice Schubart Masters; **136r** Ben Pentreath's house in Dorset; **137** Alison Hill & John Taylor's home in Greenwich; **138–139** & **140a** Chris Dyson Architects; **140b** The Walled Garden at Cowdray; **141** Chris Dyson Architects; **142a** the London home of furniture designer and upholsterer Aiveen Daly; **142b** the London home of Conrad Roeber and David Townsend who run interior design practice Schubart Masters; **143** sophieconran.com; **144–145** Alison Hill & John Taylor's home in Greenwich; **146** Ben Pentreath's London office; **147** Ben Pentreath's house in Dorset; **148l** artist Sandra Whitmore's cottage; **148r** the Kent home of William Palin of SAVE Britain's Heritage; **149** a house in Lincolnshire designed by Lulu Carter Design; **150l** stylist Karen Harrison's house in East Sussex is available for photo shoots, please contact Emma Davies on 07734 617639; **150r** & **151** a house in the West Country designed by its owners and Emma Sims-Hilditch www.theinterior.co.uk; **152–153** designed by Diana Sieff/Sieff Interiors; **153a** a house in Norfolk designed by George Carter, paint effects by Paola Cumiskey; **153b, 154** & **155b** The Walled Garden at Cowdray; **155a** Ben Pentreath's London office; **156l** painting by Taylors Interiors Ltd; **156ar** The Walled Garden at Cowdray; **156br** Ben Pentreath's house in Dorset; **157** a house in Lincolnshire designed by Lulu Carter Design; **158l** designer Helen Ellery's home in London; **158r** Chris Dyson Architects; **159** designed by Diana Sieff/Sieff Interiors; **160** a house in the West Country designed by its owners and Emma Sims-Hilditch www.theinterior.co.uk; **161al** a house in Norfolk designed by George Carter, paint effects by Paola Cumiskey; **161ar** The Walled Garden at Cowdray; **161br** designer Helen Ellery's home in London; **162al** & **162r** the Coleman's family home; **162bl** carpentry & joinery by Martin Brown, painting by Taylors Interiors Ltd; **163** designer Helen Ellery's home in London; **164a** artist Sandra Whitmore's cottage; **164b** London home of Conrad Roeber and David Townsend who run interior design practice Schubart Masters; **165a** architect William Smalley's London flat; **166al** Ben Pentreath's London flat; **166ac** Ben Pentreath's house in Dorset; **166ar** & **166b** the Kent home of William Palin of SAVE Britain's Heritage; **167** the Coleman's family home; **168–169** the London home of William Palin of SAVE Britain's Heritage; **169ac** & **169ar** Ben Pentreath's London flat; **169br** the Kent home of William Palin of SAVE Britain's Heritage; **170** Jo Berryman's home in London; **171l** Ben Pentreath's London flat; **171r** painting by Taylors Interiors Ltd; **172a** the London home of William Palin of SAVE Britain's Heritage; **172bl** & **172br** designer Helen Ellery's home in London; **173a** a house in Norfolk designed by George Carter, paint effects by Paola Cumiskey; **174l** The Walled Garden at Cowdray; **174ar** Jo Berryman's home in London; **174br** the London home of William Palin of SAVE Britain's Heritage; **175** the Kent home of William Palin of SAVE Britain's Heritage; **176** both Ben Pentreath's London flat; **177** Chris Dyson Architects; **178–179** The Walled Garden at Cowdray; **179c** & **179r** the London home of William Palin of SAVE Britain's Heritage; **180l** The Walled Garden at Cowdray; **180r** the Kent home of William Palin of SAVE Britain's Heritage; **181** & **182al** a house in the West Country designed by its owners and Emma Sims-Hilditch www.theinterior.co.uk, potboard in cellar by Neptune Classics; **182bl** the Kent home of William Palin of SAVE Britain's Heritage; **182r** the London home of Conrad Roeber and David Townsend who run interior design practice Schubart Masters; **183** the Coleman's family home; **185a** a house in Lincolnshire designed by Lulu Carter Design; **185c** & **185b** a house in the West Country designed by its owners and Emma Sims-Hilditch www.theinterior.co.uk; **186a** Jo Berryman's home in London; **186c** stylist Karen Harrison's house in East Sussex is available for photo shoots, please contact Emma Davies on 07734 617639; **186b** a house in the West Country designed by its owners and Emma Sims-Hilditch www.theinterior.co.uk; **192** a house in Norfolk designed by George Carter, paint effects by Paola Cumiskey.

BUSINESS CREDITS

Architects, artists, designers
and businesses whose
work and homes have been
featured in this book:

AIVEEN DALY
020 8962 0044
info@aiveendaly.com
www.aiveendaly.com
Pages 128–129, 142a

BEN PENTREATH LTD
17 Rugby Street
Bloomsbury WC1N 3QT
020 7430 2526
shop@benpentreath.com
www.benpentreath.com
*Pages 5, 6, 78, 80–5, 130, 131,
136r, 146, 147, 155a, 156br,
166al, 166ac, 169ac, 169ar,
171l, 176 both*

CHRIS DYSON
ARCHITECTS
11 Princelet Street
Spitalfields
London E1 6QH
020 7247 1816
info@chrisdyson.co.uk
www.chrisdyson.co.uk
*Pages 4, 138-139, 140a, 141,
158r, 177*

DOMUS
Tim Newbold
08000 93 1043
mail@domusfurniture.co.uk
www.domusfurniture.co.uk
Pages 12–13, 134

EMMA SIMS-HILDITCH
Interior design & fabrics
The Studio
The Old School House
West Kington
Wiltshire, SN14 7JJ
01249 783 087
info@theinterior.co.uk
www.theinterior.co.uk
*Pages 11, 92–97, 150r, 151, 160,
181, 182al, 185c, 185b, 186b*

Also involved in this project:
NEPTUNE CLASSICS
(laundry room furniture and
the potboard in cellar)
Lydiard Fields
Great Western Way
Swindon
Wiltshire, SN5 8UY

01793 881144
www.neptune.co.uk
Pages 11, 181

GEORGE CARTER
01362 668130
grcarter@easynet.co.uk
*Pages 15l, 22–27, 153a, 161al,
173a, 192*

HELEN ELLERY
I Love Home
Interiors and stylist
helen@helenellery.com
also:
Some of the artwork at this
location is by

ROBERT CLARKE, ARTIST
07760 296103
thedarkinterior@hotmail.com
www.blackbird.posterous.com
*Pages 105c, 112–117, 158l,
161br, 163, 172bl, 172br*

JO BERRYMAN
Interior/events design and styling
www.matrushka.co.uk
*Pages 1, 7, 41l, 46–51, 170,
174ar, 186a*

JUSTIN WEBB &
HOWARD FISHER
webb.fisher@googlemail.com
*Pages 3, 8a, 15c, 15r, 34–39,
148r, 166ar, 166b, 169br, 175,
180r, 182bl*

KAREN HARRISON
Stylist
House in East Sussex available
for photo shoots, please contact
Emma Davies on 07734 617639
*Pages 8b, 58, 60–65, 120br, 121,
150l, 186c*

LULU CARTER DESIGN
The Barn
Pulvertoft Hall
Gedney Broadgate
Lincolnshire
01406 365 300
lulucarter@fletcher-online.co.uk
www.lulucarterinteriordesign.co.uk
*Pages 9, 79l, 79c, 98–103, 149,
157, 185a*

MARTIN BROWN
Carpentry & joinery
020 7834 6747
Pages 28–33, 162bl

PLAIN ENGLISH
01449 774028
www.plainenglishdesign.co.uk
Pages 72–73, 106, 113br

PROJECT ORANGE
www.projectorange.com
020 7566 0410
Pages 40, 52–57

SANDRA WHITMORE
01403 820091
j.r.whitmore@btinternet.com
*Pages 104, 105l, 105r, 106–111,
148l, 164a*

SAVE BRITAIN'S HERITAGE
www.savebritainsheritage.org
*Pages 3, 8a, 14, 15c, 15r, 16–21,
34–39, 118–119, 148r, 166ar,
166b, 168–169, 169br, 172a,
174br, 175, 179c, 179r, 180r,
182bl*

SCHUBART MASTERS
conrad@schubartmasters.com
www.schubartmasters.com
*Pages 41c, 41r, 42–45, 136bl,
142b, 164b, 182r*

SIEFF INTERIORS
020 7730 7706
design@sieff.co.uk
www.sieff.co.uk
*Pages 120ar, 126–127, 136al,
152–153, 159*

SOPHIE CONRAN
020 7724 5318
www.sophieconran.com
with flowers by:
The Blacksmiths Daughter
Florist
Bakery Lane
Petersfield
GU32 3DY
01730 261611
Pages 66–71, 143

TAYLORS INTERIORS LTD
Painting
020 7730 3000
Pages 2, 28–33, 156l, 162bl, 171r

TESSA COLEMAN
www.tessacoleman.co.uk
*Pages 10, 59l, 79r, 86–91, 133,
162al, 162r, 167, 183*

THE WALLED GARDEN
AT COWDRAY
A romantic wedding venue with
an award winning walled garden
and café open to the public –
see website for details.
info@walledgardencowdray.co.uk
www.walledgardencowdray.com
and
ROOM IN THE GARDEN
Elegant designs in rusted iron
for the garden – plant supports,
arches, pavilions, gazebos,
pergolas & garden furniture
info@roominthegarden.co.uk
www.roominthegarden.com

Both at:
No. 1 River Ground Stables
Cowdray Park
Midhurst
West Sussex GU29 9AL
01730 816881

Also involved in this project:
THE UPHOLSTERER
15 North Street
Midhurst
West Sussex GU29 9DH
01730 810284
hello@theupholsterermidhurst.co.uk
www.theupholsterermidhurst.co.uk

Flowers by:
TIGER ROSE FLORAL
DESIGN
Bridge House
West Meon
Petersfield
GU32 1JG
01730 829989
info@tiger-rose.co.uk
www.tiger-rose.co.uk
*Pages 140b, 153b, 154, 155b,
156ar, 161ar, 174l, 178-179
main, 180l*

WILLIAM SMALLEY
Architect
07753 686711
william@williamsmalley.com
www.williamsmalley.com
Pages 124–125, 165a

INDEX
Page numbers in *italic* refer to illustrations and their captions

ACKNOWLEDGMENTS

This is the tenth book I have written or contributed to for Ryland, Peters & Small and, as always, I much enjoyed working with their excellent team including Alison Starling, Leslie Harrington, Toni Kay, Emily Westlake, Jess Walton, Delphine Lawrance, Lauren Wright and Gordana Simakovic. Jan Baldwin is equally a great pleasure to work with, and produces consistently beautiful images. I have also been greatly helped and supported by the team at Farrow & Ball, particularly Sarah Cole, Nikki Chee and Charlie Sharpley. Their enthusiasm and belief in their products is as infectious as it is genuine. One of the highlights of writing these books is meeting and speaking to the people whose houses are featured in their pages. Grateful thanks are due to all the Farrow & Ball fans whose houses have been photographed, for their hospitality and cooperation. Lastly, a big thank you to my daughter Lydia who helped me to understand the basics of visual perception.